COME BACK, MY LOVE

* * * * *

JOHN BODNAR

This book is a work of fiction. Places, events, and situations in this story are purely fictional. Any resemblance to actual persons, living or dead, is coincidental.

ISBN: 1-4107-2010-1 (e-book)
ISBN: 1-4107-2011-X (Paperback)
ISBN: 1-4107-2012-8 (Dust Jacket)

This book is printed on acid free paper.

1stBooks – rev. 04/28/03

About the Book

John Bodnar has woven a compelling and passionate tale of true love, infidelity, racism, professional jealousy, lesbianism, lust, and unrequited love against the background of a fictional college set in idyllic Carmel Valley, California.

Dean Rex Borden learned, at the age of thirteen, the qualities which have carried him through most of the delicate personal aspects of his life. This one year, however, in his professional academic life tests his resilience to put to use the hard-earned traits of obedience, patience, understanding, forgiveness, and tolerance among his diverse faculty.

Told with poignant feeling and lucid writing, Bodnar has depicted the plights of his brilliantly drawn characters with sympathetic and often deservedly scathing insight. Lizbeth glides elegantly and sophisticatedly through these pages; Gillian is caught between two worlds and almost destroyed; Traci and Rutland witness personal and professional bias in their forthcoming miscegenation; Sheila, Michael, Edward, and Sarah must work out tragic relationships; Marion and Gerald live a life of love and devotion; Jesse must look within himself for a justifiable answer to his questionable and unprofessional behavior.

And Dean Rex Borden must continue to uphold his innate qualities with complacency throughout the almost untenable situations with which he is faced.

This book
is for two people
who love me
and have always had faith in me:
my mother
Helen Bodnar Pugliese
and
my longtime partner
Wolfgang Repke

Prologue

April, 1999

CENTRAL CALIFORNIA MORNINGS IN MID-APRIL are often piercingly cold with blinding scarlet sunlight splashing across a cobalt sky. On just such a morning, Rex Borden, wearing an ankle-length green plush robe, strode across the aggregate swimming pool deck in his fleece-lined slippers. He turned up the collar of the robe and looked southwest across the landscape toward the Ventana and Pinnacle mountains; the unusual rains of the past three months— caused by El Niño—would help them to resist the early brownscorch of summer; the canyons and softly sculptured hills were lushly green.

The scarlet sun rippled in the blue water of the swimming pool and at times there was a faint orchid iridescence on the surface of the water as it spilled over the fall created by the adjacent spa.

He swung one of the white-webbed grey chairs away from the umbrella table so that he could look southeast at the mountains in the distance. With his elbows on the arms of the chair and the coffee mug held in both hands, he slipped into reverie as he often did lately— taking small sips of his steaming coffee while the reel of his life unwound one more time.

* * * * *

Four iridescent black crows lifted themselves out of the cornfield and spanned the acreage with ragged blue-black wings. They disappeared into the wispy rain clouds and left their hollow cries behind. The sun receded behind deep banks of ash-grey clouds and a cool wind rushed at twelve-year old Rex as he walked alongside his grandparents' country house.

On his left, the cornfield was alive with movement and a rustling swish. The stalks were tall and heavy with thick ears of horse corn that had burst their husks and stuck out their grotesquely large kernel-teeth at him. Coarse tassels of brown silk and yellow-green leaves trailed on the wind. Some leaves were mottled rust and seemed to bleed down their lengths. A great onrush of wind rustled the corn and a heavily-laden stalk crashed against his ear bringing pain like that of a hand across the side of his head.

* * * * *

Sister Angela stood beside him, her black habit rustling against its own voluminous folds. The rustle stopped, but the ringing in his ear left him nauseated. Stunned from the blow and its after-effects, he finally awakened to the moment. Looking up at the eighth grade nun, he cowered lower in his seat. The starched wimple stood away from her neck and vibrated—as if by magnetic wave lengths—from her uncontrollable anger. Her sterile convent smell—the unperfumed soapy cleanness—overwhelmed him. Her large pasty white hand with a gold wedding band, her mouth pinched and side-twitched in her un-Christian anger, her green eyes piercing him over the silver rim of her spectacles, her other hand clutching the chalkboard pointer: This bride of Christ towered over him menacingly. "Answer the question!"

"I...sorry, Sister. I wasn't listening," twelve year-old Rex Borden muttered. He held his hand to his ear, trying to stop the whirring noise.

"Borden," she said in her bass voice, "hold out your hands."

He took his hand away from his ear and, as he did, he saw blood in his palm. Quickly, he wiped it on his rust corduroy trousers and then held out his hands, palms up in what could be interpreted as beseeching, but which the nun saw as offered for his sin of inattention. She drew back from him and whipped his palms with the edge of the slim chalkboard pointer. At the first sting, he cried out.

"What?" the madwoman shouted. "It hurt? That was just a sample and if you flinch, young man, or turn your fingers inward, I'll beat your knuckles till they bleed. Do you hear?"

"Yes, Sister." He gulped hard, trying to hold back the tears.

She then whacked his palms twice more on the same spot; Rex felt welts rise immediately—burning, searing, scorching like fresh brands. When she finished, she said in a controlled tone, "Now, get up to the board and write, five hundred times, 'I will pay attention in school and not daydream.' And number them!"

Rex rose slowly from his seat, his hands throbbing. In the front of the room he tried to grip the chalk, but he couldn't bend his hand; red welts were blooming across his palms just below his fingers. Forcing himself to bend his hand, he clenched his teeth and finally grasped the chalk with the pulsing, blood-filled tips of his fingers. Lightly, he wrote what she had dictated. After three sentences, she was behind him—the pointer like the nose of a gun digging into the small of his back.

"Heavier," she growled between clenched teeth. "Press down on that chalk!"

Rex tried, but the pain in his palm prevented him from executing anything legible. The pointer came down on his knuckles with a thud and a crack. The chalk fell to the floor and broke into pieces. Tears welled from his eyes without a sound from his throat. He stood helpless and weak—both hands aching—his right hand useless from the sharp pain that reverberated up the bone and muscle to his armpit. He stood with his head down and his back to the class.

Sister Angela was livid. She assumed his recalcitrance to be insolence and disobedience.

"Pick up that chalk! Every piece of it! Borden, I said, 'Pick up that chalk!'"

He stooped, but the chalk was chunks and dust and he couldn't retrieve it all.

"Come with me, Borden. You daydreamer! You'll never amount to anything! God help you, when I get finished with you!"

An audible gasp from the class made her whip around, the large black rosary swinging wide at her side, the crucifix hitting the base of the chalkboard. With her palm, she swept up the effigy of the crucified Christ, kissed the figure on it, dropped it gently against her habit; through gritted teeth, she warned, "I don't want to hear one sound *from any of you while I'm out of this room." She stood for a moment glowering down her long aquiline nose through the silver-rimmed spectacles humped on it.*

Rex followed her as she whirled through the half wire-reinforced glass classroom door; leaving the door open, she fairly flew across the marble hallway to the locked visiting nurse's room. Choosing a key from her warden's ring, she unlocked the door and swung it open so fiercely that it banged against the grey filing cabinet behind it. She pulled a knock-kneed four-legged oak table into the center of the cubicle and motioned for him to lean across it. From the grey metal cupboard just beyond the door, she brought out a barber's razor strop. Standing behind Rex, she wielded the strop across his buttocks with the strength of a blacksmith. The strop hummed in the air and sang on the seat of his trousers. Three times she hit him before he cried aloud. When she was certain that he felt enough pain, she commanded: "Sit down!" Her voice resonated in the tomb-like quiet, echoing throughout the building, leaping off the granite floors, the tile and plaster walls, and intruding into the other seven classrooms where students looked at each other—fearfully aware of what Sister Angela was doling.

She designated a hard yellow oak desk chair—used by the visiting doctor—as she turned to hang the strop in the metal cupboard. Gingerly—and somewhat blinded by his tears—Rex sat down on the edge of the chair. The nun, watching him, left the cupboard and swept at him like a black hawk.

"Sit when I tell you!"

She rolled up her sleeves as if she were about to engage in a street fight, lifted him by his armpits, thumped him into the chair, and thrust her weight on his shoulders with her powerful hands. Tears rolled down his cheeks in a torrent.

* * * * *

Whenever this frequent, deep recollection ended, he jolted back to reality. He always sat motionless before he smiled and said aloud, "Thank you, Sister Angela. Thank you. I owe you more than you will ever know. God bless you and may your soul rest in peace through eternity for all the things you taught me: obedience, patience, understanding, forgiveness, and tolerance. You made me who I am and I'm forever grateful."

As he finished his now-cold coffee, he ruminated on how frequently during the years he had silently thanked Sister Angela for having taught him those virtues—even if it was at such a painful expense. "You'll have to learn," she had warned, "even if I have to beat it into you!" And she did. Thereafter, he was never caught daydreaming. As a Dean, he had to exercise extensive measures of tolerance and patience in situations with Lizbeth, Rutland, the English faculty, and Ralph Warner just this past year.

The morning quiet was broken by the ring of his portable phone on the table. He shook his head to return to the present; he grabbed the phone and pressed the answer button.

"Good morning," he said, just as a single engine Cessna took off from the local airstrip in the village below. The whirring, rising sound, ricocheting off the mountains, competed with the thin voice at the other end and made it difficult for him to hear. He instinctively stood up and turned his back to the noise.

"Good morning." It was Jesse Keller, his Chair of Composition.

"Sorry to bother you so early, but it's rather urgent that I call you as soon as possible."

Jesse told him about the automobile accident.

Rex couldn't believe what he was hearing.

"Who?"

Jesse repeated the name, "Gerald Ritchey."

"How did it happen?"

There was a pause.

"On Laureles Grade? Oh, my God!" Rex said.

"I've canceled today's classes."

"Good. And Jesse, don't say anything to anyone until I learn the particulars. Then I'll put out a memo to our faculty and the college proper."

"Traci told me the same thing until you made a decision. I haven't said a word to anyone, and I posted the class cancellations myself. Our department secretaries don't even know."

"Good. Thanks, Jesse."

Rex pushed the talk button and disconnected the phone.

Walking around the kidney-shaped pool, Rex put the empty coffee mug into his robe pocket and called his secretary at the college.

"Cheryl, I won't be in today. There's been an emergency. I'll call you when I have more to tell you. Bye."

Inside the house, from the expanse of living room window wall, he looked across the canyon at the sprawling college which had made great strides in the five years since his arrival. Classes were in session, and traffic was light on the winding canyon road. A brown UPS truck struggled up the steep macadam grade to the administration building.

He remained standing for a long moment. He really didn't want to move, but he took his coffee mug to the kitchen, then went to shower and dress.

Interlude

Chapter 1

FIVE YEARS AGO, IN MARYLAND, Rex was sitting idly in his office looking out the window during the first days of spring semester break in early March, when his secretary, Roseanne Croft, brought in the latest copy of *The Chronicle of Higher Education*—the bible of administrative educators—with a few positions circled for his attention, and laid it on his desk atop the other mail.

"Something for you in the morning mail."

He swiveled around and looked at the circled ads. She stood there and waited for him to read them. When he looked up at her, she said, "Which one will it be?"

"Wait a minute now. What are you telling me?"

"I know which one I'd like if I were you."

"I'm not looking for a job. I have one."

"You've been here what now...eight years?"

"And I've settled in."

"To the same old stuff day after day. Nothing will change here. You're young and need a challenge. Let's face it, you're just going through the motions." She sat down across the desk from him. "I've been through three deans and I could tell when it was time for them to leave. I know when the Board gets itchy. I don't want it to happen to you. I want you to leave before they look for reasons to get rid of you. You're too good to be destroyed by them. Sometimes they're so absorbed in their own mindless, political self-interests that they don't care who they destroy. I've seen them change unaccountably from praise to bitterness to destruction from one board meeting to the next, all because of state politics and their posturing for appointments."

The position in *The Chronicle* which interested him was on the West Coast.

> <u>Dean</u> <u>of</u> <u>English</u> <u>and</u> <u>Humanities</u> for new Central Pacific Coast two-year college to open in Fall, 1994. Must be knowledgeable in setting up curricula and courses. Must interview and hire entire Division of English and Humanities faculties and set up departments within the college structure. Ph.D. and at least five years' experience required. EOM. Send Vita to PO Box 359800, Monterey, CA 93940.

He worked with Roseanne to update his Vita and off it went with a cover letter in the late afternoon mail pickup.

Ten days later he received a phone call on his private line and was asked by Don Hewlett of the Valley Villa Search Committee to fly out for a personal interview with them and the Board of Trustees. He took an early morning flight out of Baltimore; arriving early afternoon, he picked up his Hertz rental car at San Francisco airport and drove two hours south to Monterey where arrangements had been made for his two-day stay at The Doubletree Hotel.

From his sixth-floor window, Monterey Bay was a frozen Pollock canvas of interlacing marine colors—sapphire, jade, cobalt, turquoise; the blinding afternoon sun starrily flickered on the white crests and plumbed its mysterious depths. The cloudless sky, a concave mantle of lapis, invertedly cupped the sea on the horizon.

After unpacking and showering, he went down to the coffee shop and had a combination sandwich and coffee. When he finished, he took out his directions to Valley Villa College which Don Hewlett had given him over the phone. From the hotel, he knew how to get back to Route 1 South; all he had to look for was the left turn onto Carmel Valley Road.

The deeper he drove into Carmel Valley, the more mountainous and rural it became. He had the feeling of new freedom without constraint or conformity; this feeling was symbolically evoked even in the various architectural designs of the houses as he drove by. Some perched at the edges of hilltops, some clung to barren hillsides on colossal stilts, others were almost hidden among California live oaks near the river. Well-kept barns; corrals; rail-fenced fields; silky-sleek, well-groomed, tail-swiping horses grazed on blue-green grass; Quail Lodge and Carmel Valley Ranch stretched moss-like golf greens on the right; a small shopping center huddled mid-Valley; the entrance to Laureles Grade yawned broadly on his left.

If the directions are right, I should be turning off the Valley Road and climbing in a matter of minutes.

And so it was.

Two miles later, he turned left and quickly found himself at the top of a canyon road and at the beginning of the estate. The monstrous ornate iron gates set in quarried stone were folded outward in an all-embracing and hypothetically welcoming gesture. He stopped his car on the road between them and got out. "I'm home," he said aloud as looked up at the gates. Far up the winding road ahead, he saw the Mediterranean complex, Valley Villa College. At first he was in awe; however, his impression changed from momentary emotionalism to the reality of job fulfillment and challenge.

* * * * *

Valley Villa College spread itself alongside a typical central California canyon. Only God could have created anything more symmetrical.

"The Villa," before it was a college, had been built by a first generation Italian who fell in love with the valley because it reminded him of the soft ranges around the Arno. He wanted to create a compound for his family because of his love for America, yet re-create something that would always be a reminder of his beloved homeland. When he finished the first four magnificent structures which stretched up the hillside—replete with a gated two-mile long Greek cypress-lined drive—he brought his family to California to show them the surprise of Renaissance art he had created for them:

orange tile roofs, beige sandstone walls, a central courtyard with a magnificent multitiered dolphin fountain, twenty-six redwood-beamed rooms with heavy mosaic work and marble sculpture. Upon their arrival, they threw up their hands, voiced their objections in vivid Italian expletives about the remote location, and returned to Italy without him. He placed the villa in the hands of Carmel Realtors and returned dejectedly to Florence. The villa remained uninhabited for several years.

When finally it was occupied, the inhabitants over the years—before the state purchased it—included renters for brief periods, an artist who bought the villa and added another building more suited to the exposure of light needed for her work, then another owner from Los Angeles who thought that he, too, could induce his family to have a "Kennedy Compound" in the middle of nowhere. He added an Olympic-size swimming pool and cabanas as well as three more buildings which labored up the hillside and lengthened the villa substantially. When this failed to induce his family to stay, he marketed it. The State of California—ever watchful for new two-year educational locations—purchased the property at a giveaway price and established Valley Villa College as non-residential and enrolled five-thousand students from Carmel, Monterey, and Salinas. The college offered two widely diverse areas of concentration: literature and computer technology. There were no other colleges on the peninsula which specialized in literature; many offered computer science, but not as in-depth as Valley Villa.

By sculpting out the hillside behind the college, student parking was created without destroying the natural aestheticism.

* * * * *

The meeting was held the next day at nine a.m. in the President's Conference Room; when Rex entered, the room seemed to be already distended with creative energy and positivism. Don Hewlett introduced Rex to the other two members of the Search Committee, the seven members of the board, President Wilson, and Vice-President Merkert. They shook hands, exchanged warm greetings, and bantered personal talk during introductions. Laughter was relaxed, chatter was soft, camaraderie was the keynote. They were all here to do a job about which they were happy; it was not a chore or a bore. Rex had never experienced such early-morning-meeting vibrancy back East; usually, there were long morning faces seated at the conference table—all wrapped in their own self-inflicted personal miseries—totally incommunicado until the presider read the agenda and the secretary passed around the attendance sheet to be signed. Ever since he arrived in Monterey, Rex felt that he belonged; now, here in this room, at this moment, he felt that the Gods of Academe nodded in assent for him and blest his arrival.

When coffee was served, Don Hewlett discussed the agenda for the day which began with the interview. Working with his Vita before them, everyone had prepared questions for Rex about his academic background at the Universities of Pittsburgh and Maryland and his innovative achievements in his current position as Dean of English at Marydale College. Luncheon was to be served in the college cafeteria during which the vice-president would make a formal presentation of the college objectives with one- and five-year plans as they were perceived at this time. After a tour of the campus, there would be a brief break; during this time, they expected Rex to prepare an overview of his day and the college itself to share with them; most importantly, the committee would like to hear how he sees his function as an active dean beyond the job description in his folder, and what fresh viewpoints and ideas he will bring to the West Coast.

Because positions for the new department had been advertised since December, they apprised Rex of the mountain of applications and folders to be read and evaluated, as well as interviews to be scheduled. Naturally, he would have all of the help he needed to complete the task. The entire committee hoped that most of the faculty would be hired by the first of July. This first summer would be a heavy work-summer; Rex said that he looked forward to the challenge.

After a seven-thirty dinner at Quail Lodge, they shook hands and parted in the paneled lobby, assuring Rex that he would hear from them one way or another by the middle of the next week, because they were eager to complete the selection as soon as possible.

In the morning, he drove back to San Francisco for a late morning flight. Getting into his car in the Baltimore airport parking lot, he had a positive feeling about the interview and was ecstatic about the

5

challenge to set up and hire an entire English and Humanities faculty. A once-in-a-lifetime opportunity! And it might be his. An administrator's dream! What another world awaited him three thousand miles to the west!

Softly, under his breath, he said, "Thank you, Sister Angela, for giving me the patience I needed to find myself at last!"

* * * * *

On Wednesday afternoon following his interview at Valley Villa College, Roseanne buzzed him from the outer office. It was Don Hewlett of the Search Committee from Valley Villa College who called to congratulate Rex as their committee's choice and asked two things: "Do you accept the position?" and "How soon can you be here?"

"Considering all there is to be done, how soon would you like me to be on campus?"

"How about two to three weeks—the beginning of April?"

"Good," Rex said.

"We'll make temporary accommodations for you until you find a house or an apartment. We'll do a real estate search and have a list for you as well as have someone take you around the area."

"Great."

"We'll see you the second week of April. We think we've chosen the right educator and we'll give you all the help we can to get you started."

"Thanks, Don."

He leaned back in his swivel desk chair and smiled, his hands steepled in front of his face, his thumbs beneath his chin.

At the prospect of a new venture and a great opportunity for a relatively young—forty year old—educator, he was as excited as a child awaiting the arrival of Santa Claus within the month.

He smiled broadly behind his hands.

Rex buzzed Roseanne. "Would you please take a resignation letter?"

PART I

In the *Beginning* Was a Party

Late August, 1998

Chapter 2

TYING HIS SILVER-AND-BLUE STRIPED TIE in front of his mirrored closet door, Rutland Jackson prepared himself for Dean Borden's annual party.

One of the things that he appreciated about himself was the fact that his hair was soft and curly, different from many African Americans, because part of his heritage was white on his mother's side. Both his great-grandmother and his grandmother had been mistresses of their wealthy landowners—the Rutlands—in Jackson, Mississippi, before, during, and after the Civil War. Secretly taken to a white family to be raised, Rutland was given a fine education at the University of Pennsylvania in Philadelphia after which he attended Notre Dame for his graduate degree and was hired as an assistant professor at five-year old Valley Villa College three years ago.

He gave the bow an extra tight tweak and fixed its dimples. He knew that he was an attractive man. He had deep, rich brown eyes— always merry and clear without any trace of hereditary bondage or innate anger to cloud them. His teeth sparkled in his deep tan face. He reminded himself of that wonderful actor, James Earl Jones—a young version, of course, because he was only thirty-four.

Now that he associated himself with Jones, he brushed his soft light brown hair, stood at the open bathroom door and saw Traci gently touching up and lightly fluffing her blond hair.

"Traci Bearse-soon-to-be-Traci Bearse Jackson, I'm ready, love. How about you?"

"Come here, you hunk."

She turned to him as he walked into the bathroom and stood before her.

"Let me fix that curl of yours. Bend down."

When he bent down, she licked his forehead and twirled a bit of hair into a curl, then plastered it flat with the palm of her hand.

He giggled and threw back his head; she pulled it forward and, as he burst into full uncontrollable laughter, she kissed his open mouth.

* * * * *

Lizbeth awakened slowly from a deep, after-sex sleep and looked at the blue figures of the digital clock. Six-fifteen. She slid silently out of bed, careful not to make a sound; Gillian was still asleep. Lizbeth looked at Gillian's partially sheet-draped voluptuousness. Her tanned plump breasts relaxed against her body; they looked like rounds of brown unveined marble. The nipples were slightly magenta from the sun. Her short brown hair was askew. Her rich, full lips were slightly parted and tempting to kiss. She lay with her hand curled on the pillow near her face, the huge, ever-present amethyst on her ring finger—except when she wore gloves for golfing—glinting in the late afternoon light.

I must get ready, Lizbeth thought.

She went into her bath, bent down, and turned the brass knob inside the sunken marble tub to a temperate zone. She unscrewed the cap on the Estée Lauder bubble bath and poured a generous dollop into the water. Although she didn't need to, she bound her feather-cut hair with wide satin ribbon from the marble vanity, and lowered herself into the sudsy water. Sighing, she slid deeper into the tub to be embraced by the warmth and bubbles. Her eyes closed, she thought about Gillian and the afternoon—of all the afternoons they had spent together since they had met on the golf course in early June.

While in deep reminiscence, she didn't hear the door open and was unaware of Gillian's entrance until she leaned forward to press the knob that stopped the flow of water. Without a word, Gillian slipped in behind Lizbeth, and pulled her close—their two bodies sliding silkily together.

Lizbeth moaned and leaned her head back onto Gillian's shoulder as Gillian pressed her lips against her neck.

"You're distracting me," Lizbeth whispered.

"What's more important than this?"

Lizbeth lifted her head from Gillian's shoulder and said, "Darling, I must get ready. I'm running late now. I don't want to be too late."

"I'll help you bathe. The least I can do in this position is to wash your gorgeous back. But let me kiss it first."

Lizbeth laughed aloud as she felt the tingle of lips touching the nape of her neck and her shoulder blades. "This will be a first for me. But, I'll take care of the rest. You can wait for me in the other room."

* * * * *

As Gillian watched from a giant, tufted-silk ottoman at the foot of the extra-wide king-size bed, Lizbeth prepared for Rex Borden's party. She slipped the champagne evening dress over her nude body; it slid into a sarong-like column of silk which clung sensuously to the curves of her body, the pencil-thin straps hugging the barely perceptible hollows of her shoulders.

On her dressing table was a large antique jewelry box which she had purchased in Florence; from it, she chose a solid gold ancient Egyptian motif chain which she had bought at Lalaounis on Mykonos.

She delicately dabbed *Shalimar* behind her ears and between her breasts.

"You *are* stunning," Gillian said.

"Thank you, love."

Lizbeth finished clipping the long chain around her neck and crossed to Gillian who took her outstretched bronze hand in both of hers and kissed it. Gillian arose and kissed the cleavage; Lizbeth leaned and touched Gillian's hair with her lips.

"I'll miss you."

11

"It will be only a few hours and then I'll be back with you where I want to be. We'll have the night."

Holding herself at arms' length, she kissed Lizbeth gently on her palely rose-painted lips.

"I don't want to crush you," Gillian whispered.

Lizbeth slid her hands inside Gillian's robe and gently cupped her breasts.

Her head back, Gillian closed her eyes and sighed.

"*You* are all I want."

Lizbeth kissed her hair.

"I could...."

"Later," Gillian said.

Lizbeth withdrew reluctantly, picked up her beaded lace jacket and evening bag from the chaise, and walked to the door. Before she closed it, she blew a kiss—with eyes closed.

* * * * *

Lizbeth Rostrand was born into a wealthy established Kennebunk, Maine, family. After two years at Barnard, she transferred to Holyoke, because she preferred to be closer to home. When she completed her Bachelor of Arts degree, her parents presented her with a year abroad as a commencement present.

She discovered England and the Continent and was introduced to a new life style with her first lesbian experience in Paris.

When she returned, she decided to continue her education and went to Harvard for a master's degree in literature. Somewhat of an Anglophile, she completed her thesis on Virginia Woolf and the Bergsonian philosophy of time, memory, and consciousness in three of Woolf's works.

Again, as a reward for her achievements and as an extension of their pride, her parents gave Lizbeth her choice of travel. She chose Russia and Greece. She went to St. Petersburg and The Hermitage; she spent a month in Greece, first to Athens, then on a tour of the Cyclades where she stayed at a dazzlingly white windswept villa on the cliffs of Syros. Of the islands, her favorite was Mykonos because of its mixture of simple Greek and cosmopolitan life and its mixture of elegantly beautiful women and seductively handsome men at play from all continents.

At home in Kennebunk, she spent her time sailing with friends, playing bridge with her family, partying, reading, sunning. On an occasional evening at one of the gay bars in Kennebunkport, she might meet a woman who would invite Lizbeth to come home with her.

She often drove to Portland—a couple of hours north—where she strolled for an hour or two, then had an authentic lobster roll on the wharf. She especially loved to walk the streets of Portland when a heavy fog rolled up the hill from the harbor and smothered the city, haloing the street-lamps at night.

* * * * *

Five years ago, she had vacationed in San Francisco. After a week at the Mark Hopkins, she rented a car and drove two hours south to Monterey and Carmel-by-the-Sea. She stayed at Spanish Bay in Pebble Beach and did touristy things: walking on Fisherman's Wharf and visiting the aquarium in Monterey, window shopping on Ocean Avenue, exploring art galleries on the side streets of Carmel, and touring 17-mile Drive at a snail's pace through Pebble Beach.

One blue afternoon, she ventured down magnificent Route 1 to Big Sur. En route, she stopped at Rocky Point Restaurant for a Bloody Mary. Sitting at a window table, she was mesmerized by the breathtaking view of the crashing, sunlit, turquoise ocean at high tide along the rocky shoreline; she continued on and had lunch at Ventana. As a result of this visually thrilling experience, she decided that the central coast of California—rather than the coast of Maine because of her love for Millay—was where she would like to settle.

At twenty-six, she knew that she wanted to make her own way without her parents' total support and meet someone with whom she could share her life. What could she do? She had graduated *magna cum laude* from Holyoke and had a Master of Arts degree in comparative literature from Harvard. Teach. Maybe she could teach.

In her elegant Spanish Bay suite, while she sipped a margarita one late afternoon, she perused the telephone directory for colleges and universities in the immediate area. She found only one two-year college listed on the Monterey Peninsula. She jotted down the number and decided to call in the morning.

After a gourmet dinner at intimate Club XIX, she retired with the latest Dean Koontz novel, *Mr. Murder.*

She awakened at eight-thirty and called room service. Until breakfast arrived, she had time for her early morning toilette and felt aglow when room service wheeled in her breakfast of freshly squeezed orange juice, coffee, and a covered dish of warm Danish. The table was set in front of the terrace door with the ocean as a backdrop. She signed the bill; the waiter thanked her and rolled the mahogany cart to one side of the room. The *New York Times* and the *Monterey Herald* were placed to the left of the table setting. She spread her napkin over the lap of her brown velvet robe and sipped the juice as she scanned the front page of the *Times*.

After she finished the *Times* and set it aside, she unfolded the *Herald*. The headline dealt with alien jellyfish entering Monterey Bay; according to all other news, nothing seemed to be happening in the world which affected this California paradise. At the bottom left of the front page was a brief, boldly underlined, attention-getting header concerning a new two-year college opening in the fall.

Continuing Update
on Valley Villa College

Valley Villa College
Opens as Scheduled

August Enrollment to Exceed 4,000

Valley Villa College, Central California's newest two-year institution, opens August 30 as scheduled.

The current enrollment for the first semester has reached 4,000, but, with three months of registration before classes convene, Ted Slote of the Admissions Office, predicts a figure closer to 5,000.

Valley Villa offers diverse degrees in Computer Technology and Comparative Literature. No other colleges on the Peninsula offer these two comprehensive degrees among their curricula.

Faculty and staff are still being interviewed.

Valley Villa College is located twelve miles west of Route One on Club Lane off Carmel Valley Road.

She finished breakfast by nine-thirty and had the operator connect her to Valley Villa College. Her call was directed to the English and Humanities Department. She introduced herself to Dean Rex Borden's secretary, Cheryl, who screened her about her educational background, arranged an appointment with Dean Borden for the next morning at nine-thirty, and gave her directions to the college which was located in Carmel Valley, about thirty miles from Pebble Beach.

* * * * *

Seated comfortably in the leather armchair, dressed in a brown silk suit, a carnelian necklace at her throat, a small handbag and gloves in her lap, feet crossed at her ankles, Lizbeth's beauty, elegance, and obvious sophistication immediately hypnotized Rex.

What a strikingly beautiful woman. How would students be able to keep their minds on their work?

"So, you're here on vacation and fell in love with Paradise like everyone else?"

Lizbeth's chuckle ended in a broad smile; she settled more deeply into the chair.

"Do you think you would enjoy teaching? These aren't Mt. Holyoke students."

"Holyoke doesn't mean they're all geniuses."

Rex pursed his lips, shook his head, and smiled as if to affirm that she could be right.

"As a student I had always wanted to be on the other side of the lectern. I enjoyed making presentations and reports in classes."

"Well, that's a good sign to start with."

Rex sat back, his desk chair locking in a tilt.

"No stage fright?"

"Never. Not even the first time in freshmen speech class."

15

"We'll be one of the few two-year colleges offering such an extensive literature program. Working with the four-year institutions, we're able to offer satisfactory courses that fit into their curricula, and thus give the student a head start in English offerings toward a major."

"A great innovation. And classes are smaller than university classes?"

"Absolutely. That's one of the advantages of a two-year college. What area of literature would you care to teach?"

"I did the majority of my work in English Literature. And, while I've traveled extensively, I'm an Anglophile at heart. So, if I have a choice, I'd prefer to teach English writers."

"I see," Rex said, "Lawrence, Woolf, Bowen, Eliot. Great writers. My favorites as well. When I discovered Lawrence and his theories about love and life and marriage, I was like a little boy forbidden to go into a particular candy store. After my first taste, I devoured every aspect of the man and his works. I had to read everything by and about him. His theories were what I needed at the time."

They both laughed.

God, Rex thought, *the physical-spiritual relationships of individuals. The clash of personalities. The totality and beauty of pairing with the right person, the horror of pairing with the wrong one. The suffering caused by staying with the wrong person for a lifetime—like an eternal penance. Unfair. Unfair.*

"Those writers are strictly university reading now. The public's taste is too pedestrian."

"What they're missing," Rex said. "But, with the proper teacher, they can be rediscovered and what they have to say can be fodder for another generation. If more people knew their work, they wouldn't make mistakes marrying the wrong persons."

They both uttered a light chuckle.

"Isn't making the mistakes all part of the process of finding the right one?"

"But sometimes passion—sexuality—speaks more strongly than sensibility."

Lizbeth displayed no reaction to Rex's in-depth musing. After a pause, however, she said, "I think we all fall into that category at one time or another."

Rex looked into her eyes. "I'm sure." Then, "Good literature has much to teach us about life."

"I was taught that literature *is* life."

He pursed his lips. "So much to read, so much to learn."

He shook his head as if he were overwhelmed by the thought of equating the quantity of reading to do versus the time left in which to read it. But that wasn't it. That wasn't it. He had slipped away. He was trying to return to the moment.

His fascination with Lizbeth was carrying him away from the interview. *As Eliot would say, "mixing memory and desire, stirring dull roots with spring rain." Dear T.S. What was it that we undergrads called him? T.ough S.hit Eliot.*

He was thinking of Lora. The Lora he lost. So long ago. Another lifetime ago. Such a stream of recollections.

What next? Are you going with anyone back East? Is it serious? No. No. Rex, what's wrong with you?

Lizbeth cleared her throat during this moment of discomforting silence.

"Where were we?"

"Literature and life."

"I think we've gone far enough down that road," Rex said.

"Would I teach only literature?"

"No. Everyone is assigned composition courses as well."

"Fine."

"When do you return East?"

"On Sunday."

"I see. So soon?"

"I've been here on the West Coast for almost two weeks."

"Is there anything you haven't seen that you'd like to see and I could show you? A drive to San Simeon on the chance that we could get tickets without reservations?"

"That's kind of you, Dean Borden."

"Rex. It's Rex if you're going to teach here."

"But I haven't been hired."

"Let's stop bantering. Even if you're not hired, you could call me Rex for the next few days."

Whoa, Rex. Slow down. Cool it, man. What's wrong with you?

She threw back her head and laughed.

17

She even laughs with elegance.

"I had planned to leave tomorrow to do some shopping in San Francisco before I left. But, thank you, for the thought and the invitation. May I take a rain check?"

Rex reached near his pen stand on the desk and unhinged and rehinged the golden figure of Sisyphus from the great boulder of brass which he had been destined to push eternally.

The ancient Greek gods were merciless and I think Sisyphus understood why he was being punished. Through Sister Angela, God is making me pay by abstinence and I think I understand. When I finally win over Lizbeth, I'll be worthy of her.

"I like that," Lizbeth said.

"A gift from my secretary when I left my last position in Maryland."

He stopped fingering the artwork. His hands lay folded on the desk before him.

"I'm happy you called and I look forward to receiving your transcripts."

Feeling that the end of the interview had come, Lizbeth stood. "I'll have them sent as soon as I return home."

Rex came from behind the desk and stood at her side reevaluating her beauty in a glance.

"I hope you won't be disappointed."

"I'm sure I won't be."

"Shall I come back for another interview?"

Don't I wish I could make you come back?

On any pretext?

"After I receive your transcripts and everything is in order, the Director of Personnel will send you all of the forms necessary to complete and return. You will hear from me or one of the department chairs about your schedule."

She held out her hand. "Thank you for seeing me. It's an exciting moment in my life."

Mine, too.

He took it and its dry warmth sent a chill through him.

What electricity. It's yours, not hers. Can she feel it? Rex, you're the one making something out of nothing. She's collected and poised as she should be.

Even as he held her hand too long, he couldn't resist touching her; he placed the flat of his left hand on the small of her back as she turned toward the door.

"Goodbye," she said.

"I hope not," he said.

"I hope not also."

But their hopes had different meanings.

And she was gone.

Rex stood with his back to the closed door, his hand on the knob behind him.

He was suddenly a young man again. Lizbeth Rostrand brought him emotionally alive once more. Oh, but at what an inopportune time. He had a whole world to create in such a short time. There would be no time for dalliance. But the time would come. Eventually. Priorities take precedence. And time. Decorum takes second place. *Patience, Rex, patience. Remember what Sister Angela taught you with that cruel lesson in the doctor's office when you were in the eighth grade? If you deserve it, you'll get it in due time.*

He laughed and said aloud, "And you got it, Rex boy, didn't you? She finally caught you reading something other than what you should have been reading. But Lizbeth Rostrand is something else to wait for. Certainly not punishment. And I hope I have the patience."

Smiling, he whistled a silly tune as he went back to his desk.

* * * * *

When she returned East and told her parents of her love for the West Coast and her decision to teach, they were happy. As always, they were happy with anything which made *her* happy. A worthy profession. Not profitable, but philanthropic in a way. And nevertheless, as true, loving parents, they reminded her that they were always there if and when she needed them.

She had her transcripts sent to Rex immediately. Within two weeks, she received a letter of acceptance for the fall semester of 1994 from the Director of Personnel.

* * * * *

There was a light knock at the door.

"Yes, dear?" he said.

The door opened slowly and soundlessly.

"You told me to let you know when it's time to get ready."

"Is it that time already?"

"It's six o'clock."

Gerald Ritchey turned from the lighted computer screen at his desk and leaned back in his chair; he removed his tortoise shell half-glasses, laid them beside the computer, and rubbed his eyes.

"It's a little dark in here."

"I hadn't even noticed," he said.

Marion switched on the floor lamp beside the desk.

Gerald looked up at her as she passed a motherly hand over his forehead before sliding it through his widow's peak of dark wavy hair.

He put his arm around her waist and buried his head against her; he felt her press his forehead into her body while she continued to stroke him as if he were a child who needed consoling.

"You need a break, darling."

"But there's no time for a break, Marion. I want to finish this before the semester begins."

"And you will."

His voice was muffled as he talked into her cashmere sweater and inhaled the lilac sachet she kept in the drawer.

"I had a good day."

She closed her eyes, nodded her head, and smiled down at him in agreement. He lifted his face and kissed her soft round breast.

She released him.

"You know…." he began.

"I know. You don't want to go. But you have to. You just don't *not* show up at Rex's reception. Forget the others. Rex is one of your greatest supporters and admirers. You were among the first faculty he hired five years ago."

"It's just those snide remarks of Jesse…."

"Haven't we always survived them?"

Gerald gave a barely audible sigh of resignation and said, "Yes, we have."

"Good. Now let's get ready."

"I love you, Marion. You're all I have."

"I know. And I love you, too. Don't forget that. You're my life."

He switched off the computer, stood up, embraced her for a minute, then pressed her body so tightly against his that he seemed to be absorbing her strength and energy by osmosis. He needed her reassurance so frequently that he often felt as if he were exploiting her. She took such good care of him. She protected him. She comforted him.

Yet, as he worked nonstop all summer, setting even tighter deadlines for himself, their personal lives were nonexistent. The only thing which mattered to her was Gerald's happiness; his wish was hers. Marion loved him and believed in him as his mother had; she made him complete.

* * * * *

After he had finished his homework and kissed his mother goodnight, thirteen-year-old Gerald overheard his father and mother in their bedroom.

"I can't help it, Eleanor. I want to be free."

"Mark, what have I done wrong?"

"Nothing. Believe me."

"Is there someone else?"

"No. Believe me, there isn't. Why would I want to leave you to be free and then find myself again—not free? No, Eleanor...."

"But, Mark, what will we do without you? We love you. Gerald needs a father during these years."

"Oh, Eleanor, please don't give me a guilt trip."

Gerald heard his mother crying as he drifted into sleep.

In the morning, after he finished breakfast and before he left for school, he kissed Mark and Eleanor as always. Without looking at Gerald, Mark turned his cheek for Gerald to kiss. Gerald put his arm around his father's shoulder, kissed his proffered cheek, and said, "Goodbye, Dad."

Mark remained unmoving. He stared at his cereal, the spoon in his right hand poised midway between bowl and mouth.

Eleanor met Gerald's lips with her kiss and gave him a hungry hug.

21

As he drew away, he said, "See you this afternoon, Mom."

When he arrived home at three-thirty, he found his mother facedown across the bed—still in her robe—weeping inconsolably.

He stretched out beside her, put his arm across her back, and snuggled his face in her hair.

Her head was turned away from his.

Her sobbing stopped.

"Your father's not coming home," she said during that breathless pause.

When he felt her body shake with silent sobs once again, he cried, too, but then he said, "I know, Mom. That's why I said goodbye to him." He added, "I overheard him talking with you last night."

She twisted her body on the bed and faced him. Her red, veined eyes were swollen, her sodden cheeks chafed and puffy.

He kissed her wet cheek and ran his hand through her tousled hair.

"We'll be fine, Mom. I'll take care of you."

"Oh, Gerald." She searched his eyes, then pressed her damp raw pink cheek against his face. With rich fervor and a smile returning to her moistened lips, she whispered into his ear, "We'll take care of each other."

Some days later, after they had fortified themselves with the assurance of each other's love, she informed him that his father was unselfish, that he was considerate enough to have left them a generous amount of money in a bank account. She insisted that Gerald not think unkindly of his father. "He still loves us. Sometimes men think they want a change, or need a change. I want you to still love him as I do."

Her inner strength propelled her to act at once to preserve the two of them. She found a smaller apartment, placed an advertisement in their Peoria neighborhood newspaper and soon had full-time day work in the surrounding area as a pre-school child-sitter for single- or married working parents.

As she did to him, he devoted himself to her. She would not be beaten; she had Gerald to live for. Mark was never mentioned again; however, he was not forgotten either.

Throughout his youth, Gerald was never permitted to say, "I can't." She told him that he *could do anything*, and she encouraged him *to do everything*.

It was kismet that he met and fell in love with Marion in their sophomore year in high school; they remained devoted to each other and their love intensified throughout his undergraduate university years.

After high school, Marion attended a two-year college and received a degree in computer science. When she graduated in the top five percent of her class, she found an excellent position as an accountant with a banking corporation. Because of her charisma and technical expertise, she was appreciated by corporate executives and earned promotion easily.

Eleanor approved of Marion and felt confident that she was the perfect woman for her Gerald. She was attractive with a great shock of shoulder-length, wavy, light-auburn hair. Her hazel eyes sparkled greenish brown when she was excited. She had a mannered poise as well as a good taste in clothes. She had been adopted when she was twelve weeks old by a totally infertile white-collar couple who loved her and treated her as their own; they also loved Gerald and were happy with him as a future son-in-law for their Marion. Eleanor knew that Marion would be a good wife for Gerald; more than that, she was certain that Marion would help him to achieve all he wanted.

When Eleanor learned that she had pancreatic cancer and that her days were counted on the heavenly abacus, she kept it from Gerald as long as possible. Her only wish—and she prayed beseechingly for it to come true—was that she would be able to be present when Gerald received his bachelor's degree in English.

Although she was pale, thin, and weak, Eleanor made it to Gerald's commencement on Marion's arm.

Before Eleanor slipped into a coma at the hospital, she asked Marion—in Gerald's presence—to promise her that she would take care of Gerald, to love him always as she did now, and to marry him soon. He needed her.

Shortly after the funeral, Gerald and Marion married and continued to live in Eleanor's apartment.

Eleanor left a small legacy for Gerald, and Marion insisted that he use it for his education; she felt that that would have been his mother's wish. She would be the provider for them until he finished his master's degree and was established in a collegiate position.

Midway in his last semester—as he was working on his thesis—a collegiate job-search committee was held on campus and Gerald applied for a position at The City College of San Francisco.

Three months later, he and Marion were apartment hunting in San Francisco.

During the first fall semester, Marion's step-parents were en route to Niagara Falls to celebrate their twenty-fifth wedding anniversary when their car was sideswiped by an eighteen-wheeler and overturned on the Pennsylvania Turnpike just before the Allegheny Tunnels. Their bodies were brought back to Peoria where Marion took care of the interment, put the sale of the house into the hands of Realtors—to be negotiated long distance—and dealt with legal affairs concerning the out-of-court settlement with the trucking firm.

Everything was completed as expeditiously as possible. She had to return to Gerald where she belonged. She knew with whom she would spend the rest of her life.

She never again returned to Peoria.

* * * * *

In their bedroom as they prepared for Rex's party, he saw that Marion was wearing a muted floral print with a narrow challis shawl which picked up the mauve shading of her dress that just covered her knees and displayed her youthful-looking, well-rounded calves which were accentuated by pumps. Unlike most of the other faculty wives, she coifed herself, and her side-swept light reddish hair with its rich highlights enhanced the fullness of her face and her delicately shaded cheekbones. Her makeup was understated, but always correct; she picked up shades from her clothes to highlight her hazel eyes.

Another of Marion's enviable traits was her smooth, wrinkle-free skin—even around her eyes. She avoided the sun and thus had the complexion of a young girl; the creaminess flowed down to her breasts; when she wore a dress that exposed teasing cleavage, Gerald was proud when he caught other men looking at the fullness of her breasts because he knew that they were his—that she was his alone.

As he dressed in his dark blue suit, he was glad that the only thing he had to worry about was a new tie; because he hated shopping, Marion always saw to it that he had a new one for Rex's party.

Standing in front of the large mirror of the dresser, he saw Marion move toward him with his coat as he adjusted his tie at the collar. She held up his coat and he slipped into it.

Looking over his shoulder, she said, "Good looking couple, I'd say. Haven't changed much since high school in Peoria."

"Yeah, grown up a bit, added a few more years—not to forget a few more pounds here and there. Even so, what's a gorgeous young thing like you doing with a tired old thing like me?"

"I don't know about that. Take a look."

Gerald was a head taller than Marion. He was pale from a lack of sun; his neat, narrow dark brown mustache had no hint of the gray that was salting his temples. He wasn't balding like some of his younger colleagues; he had tight wavy dark brown hair which he wore full on top and sculpted around his classically small ears. He was paunchless, yet he never exercised; he told her that it was inherent in him to be as trim as his father. He had a masculinely handsome face. His eyes were a deep rich brown with a little-boy wistfulness in them. His nose gave him character: It was a good English nose—full, but not broad—with a slight hump at the bridge as a result of a youthful fall. His lips were sensuously thin—one reason why he chose to wear a mustache.

"What do you think?" Marion asked.

"I think you're gorgeous and that you will make up for my shortcomings."

"And I think you're just fishing for compliments. You know what I think? I think we'll be the best looking, most dignified couple there."

She pulled his head down and kissed him tenderly on the lips.

"Let's go," she said.

* * * * *

Sarah Kendrick dragged her paralyzed legs on the carpet between her crutches, maneuvered herself through the door to her bedroom, stood just inside the door frame, and pulled the door closed. She leaned against it for just a moment, half angry and deeply hurt, before she continued across the room to her poster bed. She leaned the crutches against the perpetually turned down bed and then sat on the edge for a moment, fighting back tears and gulping the knot in her lower throat before it raised itself into a strangling pain.

In January, returning home from a faculty wives' tea-and-card game afternoon, her Ford Escort had blown a tire as she rounded a blind corner on the crest of a winding road and her car careened into a ravine. The accident shattered her legs so that she would walk with the aid of crutches—as the doctors said—maybe for the rest of her life; worse, however, she had been five months' pregnant and lost the child. In all probability, she might not be able to conceive again. "That," the doctor had said when she asked him, "will be a chancey situation about which we cannot really be positive. But let's take one healing at a time."

For months now, long after the worst weeks were over, Edward stayed away when she went to bed. Now that she was able to tend to herself, he occasionally appeared only after she undressed and crawled into bed; he would arrive and kiss her lightly on the cheek or forehead and tell her to sleep well.

How she yearned to be held for a few minutes; when he bent over her and she held on to him, she felt him stiffen and gently withdraw—as if he was afraid she would seduce him against his will.

She wanted him to lie with her and let her kiss his lips, feel his warmth next to her—even for a few minutes—put her arm across his chest and feel it rise and fall as he sank satisfiedly into sleep.

But now that she was getting stronger, she wanted him physically. Perhaps he was afraid of hurting her; had he forgotten that there were other ways for her to have him?

Sarah's fingers slowly undid the tiny fabric-covered buttons of her pale coral blouse. She hung it on the arms of the brass clotheshorse within her reach near the foot of the bed. She pushed down her magenta skirt; the waistband hugged her ankles; she used her crutch to get it from around her feet. Maneuvering the crutch, she took the skirt off the end of it, then hung it on the hanger clips below the blouse. When she unhooked her bra, her full firm breasts slid down and slightly sidewise; next, she worked off her briefs and then placed her bra and briefs on the chair by the nightstand. Not wearing stockings made undressing easier. She needed help when she wore them; but whenever she knew that Lela, the housekeeper, was not going to be around to help her undress, she never wore any. This had become more frequent, since Lela now came only during the day.

Her nightgown was folded under her pillow; she slid her hand under the cold pillow and withdrew it. Leaning against the bed, she slipped the gown over her head. The cold touch of the silky fabric alerted her nipples, and gooseflesh rippled over her body as the gown slid down.

She pulled the covers up to her neck and, with her hands under her hips, slowly worked her legs into a comfortable position beneath the covers.

She wished for Edward to come to her tonight when he returned— no matter how late it might be.

That she loved Edward with a deep, almost too-intense love, there was no doubt; she could never get enough of him—especially now after she had been deprived of him for so long. In their first years of marriage—and even before they were married—they had indulged themselves sexually and had experimented in every way possible.

He was the first man with whom she had felt so shameless about sex. He helped her to discover places on her body which she never knew existed; he could set her afire several times a night and she in turn learned that a man's body, too, offered undiscovered pleasures for him as well as for her.

Sarah ached for a fragment of such moments with Edward. She was sexually hungry for him. Lying alone in bed, night after endless—often sleepless—night, she fantasized their past lovemaking almost to the point that she was tempted to fulfill herself by her own hand. Her need was an aching one. She felt like Constance Chatterley; however, there would be no Mellors in her life to remedy her physical hunger.

Earlier this evening when he came home, she knew that tonight would be the same as every other night of the past eight months. After working in his office on campus all day doing pre-semester preparations, he rushed home, prepared her a light supper of hot French bread and chicken salad which Lela had made earlier in the day, showered, and dressed for Rex's party. He was refreshed and glowing; Edward had wonderful recuperative powers. No matter how tired he was, he could revive after a long hot shower.

27

He kissed her on the forehead as she sat in one of the wing chairs flanking the now-cold fireplace where she habitually sat to read for a few hours before bedtime. Perhaps she shouldn't have, but she reached to his crotch and held her hand there and told him how wonderful he looked and felt. He smiled, patted her head, and said goodnight; he told her not to wait up for him because Lizbeth Rostrand had invited him and a few others to her place for nightcaps and after-party conversation.

Now she lay in bed rereading Anne Tyler's *Earthly Possessions*; she equated herself with the heroine insofar as she had a desire to break away and leave everything behind—which, of course, was an impossibility.

* * * * *

Edward was doing graduate work on Evelyn Waugh at the University of Michigan; Sarah was an undergraduate working in the university library. She found the books and articles he needed for his thesis. She became, as he termed her, his personal researcher.

During the first semester of work on his thesis, they began to date and melded immediately.

They laughed about their relationship which was coincidental to Eric Segal's pair of star-crossed lovers in *Love Story* and hoped that theirs would not have the same tragic end.

They both had good, financially-firm family backgrounds: Sarah's father was a broker in Dearborn; Edward's father was in commercial real estate in Chicago.

Since Edward's thesis dealt with the use of Castle Howard in York, England, as the setting for Waugh's novel *Brideshead Revisited*, he decided that he needed on-site, first-hand research; when he asked her to join him, she did.

They found a bed-and-breakfast outside—but within a short walk—of the walled city of York.

During the next week they drove to Castle Howard daily; Edward and she had made voluminous notes which they transcribed lengthily—each night—into pages of manuscript on their table-top computers. With permission, they gathered photos of the actual rooms and some of the endless collection of artwork and Greek and Roman sculpture dating beyond 500 B.C.

Declaring themselves on holiday after their work, they went on to the Brontes' parsonage in Haworth and drove The Lake District to Wordsworth's homes. Living together as husband and wife tested their mettle as spouses and they discovered that they were ecstatically compatible.

When they returned to Manchester, Edward proposed to Sarah at the intimate Little Yang Seng restaurant. As they sipped a fine Australian white wine, they concurred that one of their great pleasures with each other was discovering good restaurants with exquisite cuisine.

"Didn't your mother tell you the way to a man's heart?"

"If she did, I don't remember. His stomach?"

"Of course."

"If that's the case, then I don't know how my mother kept my dad, because she was a lousy cook."

"There are other inducements," he said.

They laughed like two infatuated teenagers before Edward sobered abruptly and said: "And you?"

"I can't cook, but for you I'll call Julia Child for private lessons."

They decided to marry on their return to the States.

Chapter 3

THE AURA OF PARTY SCATTERED ITSELF in a confetti of cars over the broad lawn of Dean Rex Borden's home which jutted fifteen hundred feet above a canyon; from the living room, the guests had a spectacular view of a cloudless orange sunset over the Pacific Ocean twelve miles away.

In the foyer, for the faculty wives and female faculty who had brought their favorite dishes, student attendants—two male and two female—relieved them of their potluck offerings and took them to the kitchen, sometimes with verbal instructions for reheating. Rex always had student attendants who, at his request, were suggested by his faculty from their rosters of upper-class "A" students. In early August, he had his secretary, Cheryl, send out letters to the six she chose at random. If there were any refusals for one reason or another, she always had the list to fall back on. Their only requirement was to wear black slacks, a white shirt, and a black bow tie.

As his guests entered, Dean Rex Borden greeted them with extremely warm cordiality and a firm handshake. He was a sensitive man who appreciated the support and professionalism of his faculty. They, in return, admired and respected him. Each August, he held a pre-semester party as a gesture of appreciation for their dedication and for the unselfish hours—beyond their scheduled office hours—that they spent working with their students.

The pre-semester party had been instigated five years ago as a first meeting for all of the new faculty he had hired. He had had it catered from a Monterey firm but, thereafter, a number of faculty wives insisted—since he was unmarried—that they provide the food at the party. He was appreciative of their suggestion, and, after their first offerings—realizing that some of them were not exactly "gourmet cooks" and certainly not the wholesome country cook his mother had been with her natural, ingenious use of spices—he decided to supplement the casseroles with hors d'oeuvres and a few catered dishes, explaining that he couldn't permit the wives to prepare the entire menu. He explained that, since it was his affair, he felt that he needed to contribute a little something beside the champagne and wines; they smiled in agreement and also concurred—among themselves and out of earshot of their husbands—that he was one of the most charming and handsome men they had ever met. After the first three years, he learned that he was right. The fact that his catered contributions to his party were devastated, and that some contributors had to take home leftovers made him feel comfortable about his decision.

Lizbeth Rostrand arrived.

"How exquisite you look." Then he added, "As always."

She was so softly, regally radiant that, if this were another century, he would have kissed her extended hand, instead of shaking it.

"Thank you," she replied. "Rex, you're so kind and always such a gentleman and, of course, the best dean anyone could ever wish to have."

He took her proffered hand, covered it with his other one, and held it meaningfully for a moment.

"Again, thank you for the compliment."

"Sincerely spoken," she said. "I hope I'm not too late."

"Never," Rex said.

She looked deeply into his eyes, smiled warmly, and then slowly slid her hand from between his.

She said, "I'll join the crowd."

"Do."

Rex had been smitten by Lizbeth from the first day he met her. In a way, she reminded him of Lora, his ex-wife, who was blond and beautiful, too, but without the sophistication of Lizbeth. He watched Lizbeth glide off and greet people as if they were her guests. *If she was his wife, how proud he would be to share her with his guests. Did he dare to get serious with her?*

In these five years, she couldn't have missed his adulation. He had asked her to join him at several collegiate functions; she had declined because she didn't feel comfortable "dating her boss." They laughed about that. Finally, when he had asked her for a serious dinner date, she accepted. Despite the wonderful evening together, she declined further invitations because she had some previous commitments.

Thankfully—after these disappointing regrets—most of his time as dean in a new college had been spent interviewing and hiring faculty and secretarial staff, setting up departments, working with the other new deans to develop parameters and job descriptions for department heads, sitting through countless hours of meetings with the Board of Trustees, creating college-wide committees.

There had been no time for an insistent courtship. But he made up his mind this year that—since they were both still single—he would make an attempt at seriousness with Lizbeth Rostrand.

He wished that he were younger. He was forty-five and she was thirty-one. *A Chaucer May-and-December affair? Not quite. More like May-and-September.* He shook his head as if to dispel such a negative thought.

Everyone ogled Lizbeth as always; some of the faculty wives were envious of both her beauty and sophistication, while their cuckolded husbands had to give her a quick and superficial nod and never show her any particular interest.

* * * * *

"Hi, Gerald. Marion," Jesse Keller said, tilting a toast to them with a glass of Chardonnay.

Marion responded. "Hello, Jesse."

"How's the Great American Novel?"

"Almost there," Gerald said.

"Can't wait."

"You'll be among the first to know," Gerald said. Then daringly, "I'll be happy to autograph your first edition."

"Isn't this the year for your evaluation?"

"Yes."

"Perfect timing for the completion of the book, isn't it? And better for you if a publisher takes it," Jesse said with a smirk.

Gerald didn't answer, but Marion said, "It will be a hit."

"Great. Ciao." Jesse gave them a thumbs-up sign and moved off.

Edward Kendrick came by. "Good evening, Marion. You look lovely." He nodded to Gerald. "Gerald."

"Thank you, Edward." She smiled at him. "How's Sarah?"

"Coming along quite well, thank you. Of course, she has bad days, but we're happy with her progress."

"That's good. Would it be all right for me to come by some time? I haven't been to see her for a while, and I'd really like to visit."

"You're such a good Samaritan, Marion. Of course it would be all right. I know she would love to see you. Give her a call any time. As you know, she's always home." This was not said sarcastically.

"I shall."

Edward moved away.

With a towering six-branched rubber plant reaching into the vaulted ceiling as their backdrop, Gerald and Marion stood watching the crowd in the masculinely appointed room. People were seated in the brown Knoll Plattner chairs; on pillows on the raised Mexican tile hearth with heavy, solid brass andirons against a brass mesh screen; on the textured velvet sofa; and on the floor around the Florence Knoll half-inch glass coffee table—the centerpiece a huge bowl of green crystal which Rex had bought in Copenhagen one summer. Others stood near the bar. A student watched from behind the bar and whenever anyone's glass looked a bit low, he quickly left his place behind the bar and refilled it with either champagne or the wine they had chosen. Other student-waiters periodically passed hors d'oeuvres and cloth napkins; each hors d'oeuvre platter was then placed around the huge sculptured silver dish from Cabo San Lucas on the round glass-covered Carrara marble table in the solarium dining room.

"Edward is always a perfect gentleman and host, isn't he?"

"Yes, he is. One of the few."

A young man in his late twenties, who recognized Gerald, came up to them. He was obviously overwhelmed by the whole affair and was in awe of being in the same room with so many professors.

"Hello, Professor Ritchey."

He extended his hand.

"And your name?"

"I'm sorry. Milton Bream. I'm new to the department this year. You were among the professors who interviewed me as an assistant professor last spring."

Gerald shook it. "I remember now. My wife, Marion."

"I'm pleased to meet you. Forgive my embarrassment. I'm a little lost right now."

"Don't I remember when once I was?" Gerald said.

Milton smiled and chuckled. "You're kind."

"No. I'm honest."

"Thank you for the reassurance. I'm afraid I need it in this company."

"Let me give you a word of advice. No company should make you insecure because, often, many of those in that company are less secure than you."

"I guess a word from the wise is a good word of advice. Again, thanks."

He lifted his wine glass in a toast to Gerald, then sipped.

"Isn't Professor Rostrand elegant? Every movement of hers is grace personified. She looks as if she just stepped out of the pages of *Vogue*."

They agreed.

Lizbeth was standing sidewise talking with Traci Bearse and Rutland Jackson; there was an aura surrounding Lizbeth. She exuded old money and everything that was associated with it. Her demeanor, her East Coast sophistication, the way she sipped her drink from the flute, the light toss of her silky champagne-blond head when she laughed, her ability to discuss any topic in conversation, her charm with men. Even her students were in love with her: The young men flocked to her office on the pretext of needing special help; the girls were entranced with her sophistication and were staggered by her elegance. And she was cool. Nothing ruffled her.

35

When Rex moved through the room—there were at least forty people—everyone stopped him and made small talk. Some of the faculty wives had to touch his arm when they talked; they even took on a new glow in his presence.

He finally made his way to Gerald and Marion.

"You three look so lonely over here."

Rex extended his hand to Gerald, then to Milton.

"Milton Bream, sir, a new faculty member this fall."

"Welcome to Valley Villa, Milton."

"My pleasure, sir. We were just commenting on Professor Rostrand's beauty."

Rex turned and looked. "She has that," Rex said, "and talent of the same caliber."

"We know," Marion said.

Rex faced them again. "Marion, you're quite a beauty yourself."

He sipped his wine and tipped his glass to her.

Marion blushed deep into her cleavage and self-consciously adjusted the challis shawl. "Rex, you always know the right thing to say. Thank you. I guess for an aging...."

"I tell her that all the time," Gerald said, "but she never believes me."

Marion touched Gerald's shoulder, then squeezed his arm.

Gerald leaned down and kissed her lightly.

"It's wonderful to see your devotion to each other. Milton, you're in good company."

"Yes, sir, I realize that."

"The City College of San Francisco's loss was our gain when Gerald came to us."

Gerald and Marion smiled at each other.

"How's the book coming along, Gerald?"

Gerald knew his question was sincere. "I'm almost finished with the last revision, and then it goes off."

"Do you have an agent?"

"No. Some of the textbook representatives have offered to take it back with them and give it to a fiction editor at their firms."

"Wonderful," Rex said, "You couldn't ask for a better inside connection. I wish you luck. How long have you been working on this and teaching a full schedule, too?"

"Almost six years. I started it before I came here."

"Must be a biggie."

"Close to thirteen hundred pages."

"Wow! Another *Gone With the Wind*," he said.

"Not quite as long. I only hope it sells a fraction as well as Mitchell's has."

"So do I. But you won't leave us, will you, if it does?"

"After Marion, teaching is my life, And I love this area, this college, and my students. Never. Don't worry about that. All I'd like to do is give Marion more out of life."

"Gerald! There's nothing wrong with my life as long as I have you." She hugged him.

Again, he leaned down and kissed her lightly.

"Take a lesson, Milton, and hope you find a mate who will be as devoted to you and share your love as they share theirs. They've been lovers since high school in Peoria. That's a rarity. And she didn't even lose him when he went through his degrees at the University of Illinois. Some academicians—when they're married and working on degrees—often end up losing their partners because of the time needed to devote to their studies."

More hors d'oeuvres were offered. Smoked salmon topped herbed cream cheese on a thin English cucumber slice.

"The hors d'oeuvres are heaven, Rex."

"Thank you, Marion. They're made by the caterer at Tarpy's on Route Sixty-Eight near the airport. Have you not eaten there?"

"We go to dinner on rare occasions. Birthdays. Anniversary. The holidays. Otherwise, we eat at home. Gerald loves my cooking," she said.

Another tray of hors d'oeuvres was passed. Caviar on chopped egg and minced sweet onion: all on a savory thin wafer.

After they popped them into their mouths and finished eating, Rex said, "Tell you what. As soon as Gerald finishes the revision and the book is hauled off by one of the book representatives, you'll be my guests at a celebration dinner at Tarpy's."

Marion and Gerald looked at each other and smiled.

"A deal? Shake on it?"

All three shook hands. Rex also shook Milton's hand as he said, "I'd better see how things are in the kitchen and then move around a bit. I want dinner served at eight. Not too early, is it?"

"Perfect time," Marion said. Of course, she didn't tell Rex that they usually ate around six o'clock.

When Rex left, Milton said, "I don't think I should monopolize you."

"Not at all," Gerald said.

"On the other hand, maybe I should mingle more. Although, to be honest with you, I'd rather stay with you because I'm a little nervous."

"Don't be," Marion said. "There's nothing to be nervous about. They're people just like you."

"Thank you, Mrs. Ritchey."

Gerald placed his hand on Milton's shoulder and shook it gently before he let it drop to his side.

"Some fatherly advice, Milton," he said. "You're fine. And I know you'll be a good teacher. You wouldn't be here if all of us on the search committee hadn't felt that."

"I feel that, too, Professor Ritchey. It's just that I'm new and everyone here is established."

"Everyone is always new somewhere, Milton. They've all been where you are. I was new five years ago. Confidence, Milton, confidence."

Marion extended her hand.

Milton took it.

"Mrs. Ritchey, it has been my pleasure to meet you."

"Thank you, Mr. Bream. You're a fine young man, and you'll find your niche here. The students will love your youth. And I'm certain you'll find them just as eager to learn as Professor Ritchey does."

Milton smiled.

"You know, Mr. Bream, you remind me of Professor Ritchey when he first started to teach. You have that same sensitive manner which, by the way, is good. I have no doubt that you'll be a success in the classroom."

"I feel better already," Milton said.

"If I can help you in any way, come to my office, will you?"

"I promise, Professor Ritchey."

"Good."

Milton moved into the crowd.

Traci, Lizbeth, and Rutland approached them just as Milton left; they greeted each other with kisses.

"Great evening as usual," Rutland said.

"Never fails," Gerald said.

"So, how are the happy lovers?" Marion asked.

"Happier as each day goes by," Traci said and chuckled.

"To wedded bliss soon," said Lizbeth.

The three of them lifted their glasses and toasted Traci and Rutland who beamed at each other.

When they finished, Rutland said, "We'll drink to that, won't we, love?"

"You bet," Traci said.

They clinked their glasses, drank, and kissed.

When they separated, Rutland said, "Hmm. Almost as good as the wine."

Traci jabbed him playfully in the ribs. Winking and looking directly at Lizbeth, she said, "He'll pay for that when we get home."

With his free hand, he pulled her close and said, "I hope so."

They all laughed.

"How was your summer, Gerald?"

"Oh, Rutland, you know Gerald's been intent on finishing his novel. He worked harder at it than he would if he had been teaching summer courses."

"Certainly more rewarding and less frustrating, Marion," Rutland said. "Summer courses are often not satisfactory for the students or the professor."

"How was Maine, Lizbeth?"

"Wonderful, Marion. But I'm always happy to return to Paradise. More so than ever this year."

From Marion. "Oh?"

"I guess I've found different interests here than I had had before."

"Sounds romantic," said Gerald.

"Come on, Lizbeth, share," Traci urged.

Lizbeth just smiled.

"Who is he?"

"I don't kiss and tell, Traci," Lizbeth said as she sipped the last of her drink.

"Professor Rostrand." The bartender was at her elbow with another flute from his tray.

"Thank you," she said, surrendering her empty one.

"I bet it's Rex."

"I never thought of that, Traci," Marion said, "but wouldn't that be great!"

Lizbeth looked up from the rim of her glass as she sipped. From deep within her came a soft chuckle. "Stop," Lizbeth said, "you're making me blush."

"Maybe we could make it a double wedding," Rutland said.

"A toast," Traci said, "to a double wedding." She looked at her glass. "But it's empty," she said, "I hope that's not a bad omen." She signaled the bartender who arrived promptly and filled their glasses. Each thanked him as he poured.

"Okay. Now."

"I won't drink to that," Lizbeth said, shaking her head, her soft waves dancing.

"Why, Lizbeth?"

"Gerald," said Lizbeth, looking up at him, "I'm superstitious."

"You think that that might cancel him out?"

Lizbeth didn't respond; she just shook her head and sipped her brut.

"I can understand," Gerald said.

"Well, you all just drank to Rutland and me," Traci said, "Do you think that will cancel us out?"

"Nothing, but nothing," Gerald said, "could quench that blond inferno!"

Their laughter was interrupted when a waiter came and announced that the buffet was served.

They set their glasses on the coffee table. Marion and Lizbeth each linked an arm through Gerald's arms and followed Traci and Rutland into the dining room.

* * * * *

40

When Lizbeth arrived home, she found Gillian in a robe curled up on a sofa in the library thumbing randomly through the new Tom Wolfe volume.

"Hi, I'm back."

Gillian closed the book and laid it on the sofa beside her.

"I'm glad. I can't get into this. Certainly nothing like his last one. *The Bonfire of the Vanities.*"

Lizbeth went to her, bent down, and kissed her upturned lips.

"How was it?" Gillian asked.

"Delightful as always. Next year at this time, I'll take you with me."

"Won't that be a revelation?"

Lizbeth placed her handbag on the dark cherry coffee table, then slipped out of her jacket and laid it on the arm of the sofa as she sat down opposite Gillian.

"Can I get you something to drink?"

"Yes, thank you. Sherry. But I can get it."

"You just sit."

Gillian went to the wet bar in the far corner of the room. In the mirrored wall behind the glass shelf, as she reached for two glasses, she saw Lizbeth settle deeply into the sofa. She turned and set the glasses on the bar, removed the knobby crystal stopper from the heavy Orrefors decanter, and poured the syrupy amber liquid into them.

"Were there many people?" she asked as she stoppered the decanter.

"The usual number. About forty including three new young faculty."

Gillian took the drink to Lizbeth and curled her leg under her as she sat.

"To the evening," Lizbeth said.

They sipped and kissed.

"You're sure your parents are all right tonight?"

Gillian drew closer to Lizbeth and put her arm across the back of the sofa behind Lizbeth's head. She ran her fingers through Lizbeth's soft hair.

"They were watching TV when I called. They said they were going to bed early."

41

"Your father is so young to have had a heart attack."

"It's as the doctor said. When some men retire, they can't handle the sudden stop of pressure and the fast pace they've been accustomed to all of their lives."

"There's a terrible irony in that, isn't there? You work all your life to retire and then you fall apart because you stop working."

"Mother takes good care of him when I'm not around. They love each other very much. I'm just happy it wasn't worse."

"Do you miss working a full-time job?"

"No. But I don't like not knowing the days and hours they'll want me to work."

"I don't mind, as long as we have as many hours together as possible. Actually, I need time, too, through the week to do things. If...."

Gillian pulled away, uncurled her leg, and knelt on the edge of the cushion to face Lizbeth.

"Go on," said Gillian, "If what?"

"If it was possible for you to live with me, it would reverse the situation. I mean, you'd live here and you wouldn't have to work, but you could go to your parents and stay as you're needed. But you'd always come back to me."

Lizbeth emptied her glass and set it on the table.

Gillian did the same, then said, "Maybe some time. I'd have to broach it slowly."

"I know."

Lizbeth brushed her lips against Gillian's.

"Let's call it a night while there's some left."

They rose.

Gillian took the glasses to the bar. Lizbeth, jacket and handbag in hand, was already out the door. Gillian switched off the lights and followed Lizbeth to the bedroom.

* * * * *

Edward Kendrick was one of the last to leave the party at ten-thirty. The moonless sky was freckled with blue stars. Even before he reached his black Honda Accord, he knew he wasn't going home. He knew it when he told Sarah that he might go to Lizbeth Rostrand's for a get-together after the dinner party. There was no invitation; it was pure invention on his part. And Sarah would never know anything different. He was safe and he knew it.

When he came to Valley Road, he turned left. The village was quiet at this hour, except for The Running Iron. The restaurant side was empty because they had stopped serving, but the saloon was in full swing; the voices and juke box country-western music carried across the road and into the night. Beyond Via Veneto, he turned right onto Robles del Rio road, crossed the river at Rosie's Bridge, and then turned right and wound up the hill. In ten minutes he'd be in heaven. He chuckled at the pun.

* * * * *

Twenty-year-old Sheila Mercer stepped out of the shower and stood looking at her slender nakedness in the full-length door mirror as she dried herself. She took off her green bath cap, hung it on the shower head, closed the glass door, shook her head so that her shoulder-length hair fell into a wavy cascade of rich burnished copper fullness. From the sink countertop she took a purple atomizer and sprayed her body with Elizabeth Taylor's *Passion*. He loved it. He had given it to her. He was the only one for whom she wore it.

She wouldn't wear it even for Michael, her well-endowed classmate stud, although she should have because of the musty odor of his clothes which clung to his body. The first time she went to bed with him was at his rented house on the river; even the sheets were musty to the point that she was so distracted by the smell that she almost could not complete the sex act. She noticed Airwicks everywhere, but evidently they were not strong enough to dispel the mustiness. That was the first and last time she had had sex with him at his house; thereafter, she took him home, made him shower and shampoo his hair, gave him her deodorant, had him spray his face and body with Pierre Cardin after-shave which she had bought for him at Longs Drug Store, and then let him make wild love to her.

There was no doubt about his greatness in bed. His size alone satisfied her as it filled her. And when she lifted herself off the bed to meet him as he thrust his full length hard-on into her, he jammed his open mouth onto hers and forced his similarly hard, elongated tongue

43

into her throat to stifle her screams during her orgasm. She bucked wildly like a stallion in the first throes of captivity, and he reacted with the controlling fierceness of a First Prize-winning bronco buster. Not once, but at least three times during each session. She was almost insatiable. When she saw him on campus, she wanted to tear off his clothes and do it on the spot in front of everyone so that they could see what a hunk he was.

She put on her green robe, slipped into her matching satin slippers with feathery pompoms, and went into the living room to wait for him.

The searchlight effect of the car lights swept the room as the Accord swung down from the main road onto the gravel driveway.

Edward had arrived.

* * * * *

Driving down pitch-dark Robles del Rio road at one-thirty in the morning, Edward could smell Sheila on his body. *Passion* in all ways. His mind switched back to the fourth week of the past spring semester when their affair began.

When he came into the classroom Monday morning with the corrected tests, there was an audible groan. As was his habit, he wrote the test score range on the chalkboard with the number of people who achieved in each range. There was another groan—of delight this time—when they saw that there was nothing below a seventy. When he taught, he walked up and down the aisles; he did the same when he distributed the Early American tests they had taken on Friday. He returned the "A" papers first. Sheila had earned a ninety-nine, and when he handed her the paper, he said, "Great test." She took the paper, looked up at him—directly into his eyes—and, with a warm smile, she licked her lips and said, "Great teacher." She held his eyes for a moment too long and he felt a stir of warmth below his belt— something he shouldn't have. After he returned all of the papers, he went to the lectern. Looking into the class, he saw Sheila leaning across the aisle to a sulky Leonardo DiCaprio-like young man in his early twenties. He called roll and watched who answered. Michael Larson. He had gotten an eighty-one.

At the end of class, they left the room together but, as she passed, she gave Edward an adoring look and said, "See you soon." to which he responded, "On Wednesday, for sure."

Over her shoulder, she smiled as she winked and said, "Maybe sooner."

On Tuesday, he had only one class. At eleven o'clock, he was on the telephone in his office, when he saw her pass the open door. She looked in, but didn't stop. When he finished, however, she entered—after a calculated time.

She was wearing a tight mini-mini-skirt under which there was nothing. He could almost detect the thrust of her pubic region. She wore a pale blue sweater and she was braless; her nipples were lovely points. The sun issuing through the slats of the Levolor shades behind him put burnished highlights in her copper hair. She was attractively made up—as always, even for class—and her metallic-red painted lips were Locklear lips—sensuous and exciting.

Edward would have risen to greet her but he had a sudden, instant erection. Actually, he thought by way of a justifiable excuse, it isn't necessary for a professor to rise to greet a female student.

"Professor Kendrick, I hope I'm not interrupting," she said.

"My door is always open."

"I just had to tell you that I love your class. As I said when you returned my test, you are a great teacher and you made those dull Puritans interesting. Probably the best professor I've had so far, but then I haven't had many—in the Old Testament sense, that is."

She chuckled and looked down, then up quickly to see his reaction.

"I don't want you to think I'm saying that in order to get a grade."

Her obvious allusion to the Old Testament did not elude him, but he ignored it and said, "That never entered my mind and could never happen. What anyone earns is what she gets."

"Good," she said. "I have other classes where I can feel that the professor plays favorites."

She stood in front of the desk now, pressing herself against it so that her tender flesh shelved itself on the edge of the desk.

His erection throbbed.

"Won't you sit down?"

He motioned to the chair at his left.

She dragged the chair to the front of his desk, far enough away for him to get a good glimpse of her body. She sat with her legs closed, but the skirt rode almost to her hips—or so he thought.

"May I put my things on the edge of your desk? They'll fall off my lap."

"Of course."

As she rose, he glimpsed what was under her skirt; she was truly burnished copper. His erection throbbed against the bottom of his center desk drawer.

She saw him look and gave him a shy smile before she returned to the chair.

"I do hope I'm not taking up your time."

"You're not. I have no appointments scheduled and I was just getting ready to leave."

"I am, too," she said.

"Where do you live?"

"On the shady side of the valley. I have a lovely garage apartment. Very private."

"I've been to the Ridge Restaurant over there. A lovely view of the village."

"I live just below it."

"Then you should have a good view also."

"The road I live on is aptly named. Robles del Rio. There are oak trees blocking my view of anything but more oak trees."

"What a pity."

"I have to create my own entertainment."

Edward felt that this was an opening of some sort and threw out a suggestive comment.

"And what sort of entertainment?"

"I have a great CD collection—from country-western to classical. I don't watch much TV. And, then, of course, there are men."

Edward was taken aback for a minute; his erection hurt under the desk.

"Do you have a steady boyfriend?"

"Not really steady. He sits next to me in class. He thinks he is, but I'm always looking for someone special. We have good sex."

Gulp.

Throb.

Throb.

He put his hand under the desk for a moment and adjusted himself.

She caught him, looked away, then back, and smiled.

"Do you come to the college by bus or do you drive?"

"I commute with someone else who lives just up the road from me."

An opening.

"Well, if you'd like, since I'm leaving and you're ready to go anyway, perhaps I could take you home."

"Oh, I couldn't let you do that." Then, "Do you live out my way?"

"No, I live on Highstep out the Valley Road toward Carmel. But it's no problem."

"You're sure?"

"I wouldn't offer if it was. But what about your ride?"

"No problem. If I'm not at our appointed meeting place at the usual time, she knows I've gotten another ride and she leaves."

She stood up.

The skirt was tightly wrinkled from sitting and had crawled up permanently. She reached down and tugged at the hem to lengthen it; it remained wrinkly short. She took her books and notebook from the desk.

"Give me a minute," Edward said.

"Take all the time you want. I'll wait."

He reached beside his chair for his attaché case, placed it flat on his desk, snapped it open, and put in his literature book and his roll book. As he stood, he upended his attaché case on the desk to block his tented crotch.

She turned and he followed. Slowly, as he walked, his erection subsided, and he could feel moisture on the inside of his thigh.

That was the beginning.

As they drove, she asked if he was married.

"Oh, I'm sorry. I didn't see your wedding band."

A lie. How could she not have seen it? At the lectern during the semester. In the office. Should he tell her about Sarah? He was this far.

"In January, my wife had a car accident. She lost our baby and she...."

47

"Oh, how tragic."

"It's a bit difficult, but we have a housekeeper-cook who takes care of her and everything for us."

She was silent for the rest of the drive up Robles del Rio.

Winding up the road under over-branching oaks, he wondered what the next step would be.

"Here we are. Take the next left."

He drove down a steep incline, parked in front of the double garage, and turned off the engine.

"Won't you come up for a glass of wine?"

"I shouldn't."

"That's the least I can offer you."

Good line. Suggestive.

"Are you afraid I'll bite?"

Didn't he wish.

"No, I might."

What a game! Why not go in and fuck her? That's what she wants. But I've never touched a student and, though I'm tempted, I shouldn't.

She laughed.

"Why don't you come in, see the apartment, and let me see how dangerous you are."

"Okay. Why not?"

He laughed nervously.

She led him to a stairway alongside the garage. Looking up as she walked ahead, he could not see anything, but his mind worked evilly.

The door was unlocked. They entered a small kitchen. Everything was bright yellow and white—exuding a sunlit atmosphere—and meticulous; there wasn't even this morning's coffee cup on the drainboard—if she drank coffee. She led him into the living room. Again. Order everywhere. There were a sofa, two chairs, a low bookshelf, a vividly colored reproduction of Van Gogh's Sunflowers, a desk and chair where she obviously studied, and a small fireplace.

Small talk.

"That's a beautiful reproduction of the Van Gogh. I've never seen such brilliant colors except in the original."

"Oh, Thank you. It's mine. Probably one of the few things that aren't included in the rent."

As she walked to the desk and placed her school paraphernalia on it, she said, "Make yourself comfortable."

Turning around, she asked, "Red or white?"

"What?"

"Wine."

"Oh. Red."

He watched her rear movement as she walked toward the kitchen.

She returned with two glasses of red wine.

"It's not Frog's Leap, but it's a good Gallo Cabernet."

"To you," he said.

"To us."

They sipped and she placed her hand between his legs as she leaned over and kissed him.

* * * * *

He was nearing his driveway.

The house was dark.

He pressed the garage door opener above the rear-view mirror and one door of the double garage slid up noiselessly. He walked past the laundry room into the kitchen, turned on the light, took a double old fashioned-glass from the cupboard near the sink, and filled it with ice from the freezer. As he left the kitchen, he flicked off the light switch. Walking through the living room in the dark, he stopped at the bar and poured himself a generous nightcap of Dewar's.

On the way to his room, he saw a light under Sarah's door and tiptoed past it.

Chapter 4

THE SECOND WEEK OF SEPTEMBER, almost three weeks into the fall semester, the textbook representatives arrived on campus. Gerald was in his office when the Parthenon Press representative appeared in the doorway.

"Happy semester!"

Gerald looked up from his desk. When he saw who it was, he stood and smiled.

"Thanks, John."

John Stanton extended his right hand as he approached—a large book bag in his left—and Gerald thought of Willy Loman as he must have looked in his youth. Trudging from city to city but with his bookwares. Poor Willy Loman, America's tragedy. Except that John was not Willy Loman or America's tragedy. Not at the price of textbooks these days. And John had been a book representative all of his life, so he could rely on his regular customers for repeat sales when the texts were revised or when new texts superseded the old with new methodology. Gerald was not envious of his life; he thought of all the lonely times on the road that John and other reps spent away from their families.

And he could go home to Marion every night.

"Great to see you. How was your summer?"

"Super. We spent a month on the Cape as usual. And yours?"

"Well, since I didn't teach this summer, I had plenty of time to work on my book."

"How'd it go?"

"Finished it." He said this softly and with a gentle smile as he looked up at John from under arched brows—not with triumph, vanity, or relief, only shy pride.

John set down his bookbag and took Gerald's hand again.

"Congratulations!" This was said sincerely, with the broadest smile any man could give at his happiness for another man. Then he added, "You haven't sent it to anyone yet, have you?"

"No."

"You remember what I said."

"Yes."

"Good."

On that note, he sat in the chair facing Gerald. Settling in, he continued. "Do you have it here? If so, I'll take it with me today."

"No, of course not."

Gerald sat, too.

"Well, I'll be spending three days on campus and I can drop back tomorrow or Thursday."

Gerald smiled shyly. "I'll bring it in tomorrow. In case you don't get a chance to stop by tomorrow, I'll lock it in my file cabinet so I have it when you *do* come back."

"Great."

They then settled into the business of spring book selection as John withdrew new- and revised texts from his bag.

* * * * *

Edward Kendrick sat at his desk, leaning back in his chair, his hands folded prayer-like just below his nose, his fingertips touching. Horizontal bars of light from the tilted Levolor shades scarred the ceiling above him.

The summer was gone; the trysts had been easy. He had taught two morning courses and on the pretext of working in his office, he spent a few hours of every afternoon with Sheila. She had taken summer courses and had met him at his car at noon. They had a hamburger outdoors at The Running Iron or a croissant sandwich in the lovely shaded garden at The Summerhouse. Students did not frequent either place. Most students left the college after their classes and went to jobs which supplemented their spending money or helped them to accrue money for fall tuition. Edward and Sheila had been safe all summer.

Edward learned the truth about Sheila. She was from Monterey. Her family owned a business supply store which was highly competitive with other stores of the type on the Peninsula. She had lied about not owning a car; she had a black Fiat Spyder in the garage below her apartment; she had set out to seduce him that day by having a friend drive her to the college. She had chosen Valley Villa College because of its situation and because she wanted to be away from home. Valley Villa College was small; she could have gone to Santa Cruz or San Jose, but she didn't want to be in a city of any size.

She told him about Michael Larson and their relationship; she said it was pure animal sex; he couldn't help but wonder why, then, that she chose him. She told Edward she loved his mind and his maturity.

"After all," she said, "don't girls usually have an interest in their professors? Some even fall in love with them because of their minds." She added, "But, of course, they have to be handsome, too." She told him that she loved his experience in sexual matters; he was not solely interested in a quick orgasm—or several quick orgasms. It was Edward's mature foreplay that she loved. She loved his hands playing over her body, titillating every inch of her and teasingly bringing her close to an orgasm several times before the real one which "made planets collide." She loved the ripeness of him, the mature fullness of his penis; it was so different from the eager pink-and-white rod of a youthful one. She told him it was smaller than Michael's, but more gently aggressive and satisfying. Far more so. Like a gentleman with a lady, not a boy with a whore. He was not Priapus as was Michael, but a Greek god showing tenderness which, of course, was a contradiction—especially with Apollo and a few other vengeful Greek gods who ravaged innocent virgins.

They had enjoyed walking barefoot on the beach at the foot of Ocean Avenue, exploring art and sculpture galleries and eating in out-of-the-way places in Carmel, driving to Big Sur and dining on the

53

terrace at Ventana, having him talk about Henry Miller before and after they visited the museum below Nepenthe where they had eaten Ambrosia Burgers. For him it was a summer of youthful resurgence; for her it was an escape and a rich fulfillment of her greatest fantasy.

One spectacular afternoon, after stopping along the cliffs of Route 1 to experience the excitement of the coast, they drove to Lucia and had lunch. Lucia was a few cabins, a gas station, and a tiny, intimate restaurant suspended on a cliff over the Pacific. He remembered this specifically because—overwhelmed by the scenery—she wanted him to rent a room and spend the afternoon in total absorption of each other.

Instead, they drove back to her place where they lay rediscovering the pleasures of the bodies they already knew so well. He never said he loved her and she never expected it. He understood what she loved about him: his mind, his maturity, his gentleness. She was lying on her side, her elbow bent, her head propped in her hand, her body pressed against his, her breast resting on his chest. Her left hand ran up and down his body.

He asked her about Michael.

"He calls."

"Do you see him?"

"Do you mean do I have sex with him?"

He didn't answer.

"Do you and Sarah have sex?"

"We haven't since her accident. And...there's you."

"Isn't she suspicious?"

"Is Michael?"

"You didn't answer me."

"Does it matter if she is?"

"Certainly not to me."

"Isn't Michael suspicious? You had a regular affair with him."

"I tapered off so he wouldn't be, but he's still inquisitive. He asks me questions about how I spend my time when I'm not with him. About why I don't want sex as often as I used to. Why I've cooled off."

"And?"

"I told him I don't feel the need like I used to."

"He bought that?"

She shrugged. "I guess."

She kissed him lightly, stopped her hand where it would be most effective, and said, "Let's not talk about Michael. Let's take advantage of *now*."

Throughout the balance of the summer they never spoke of Michael or Sarah again.

* * * * *

Rutland Jackson closed and locked the door of his office. On his way to meet Traci for lunch, he passed Gerald's office. The door was open, but he knocked.

Gerald looked up.

"Come in," he said.

"I'm glad I caught you before you left."

"Won't you sit for a while?"

"Traci's expecting me. Won't you join us for lunch? We're having a bite in the cafeteria."

"Thanks, but Marion's expecting me. I'll take a rain check."

"How's the book?"

"Finished and gone."

"Congratulations," Rutland said with genuine honesty. He shook Gerald's hand. "My best wishes for its success. You deserve it."

"Thanks. I'm a little lost now."

"I know how you feel. When I finished my critical biography of John Edgar Wideman, I felt the same way."

"When is it due?"

"The first week of October."

"Can't wait to read it."

"You get an advance copy as soon as I receive my author's copies."

"Thanks, Rutland. I'll do the same for you when it happens."

"It will. Got to go now. See you later."

Gerald liked Rutland. As he sat down and watched him leave, he mused about the number of colleagues who were openly opposed to Rutland's affair with Traci because of their racial difference. His grandmother used to say that "it doesn't matter who you fall in love with as long as you love each other. Poor, rich, ugly. Love can fall in a dung heap. It's no one's business."

Rutland and he had been friends for three years, ever since Rutland was hired and Gerald was appointed his faculty mentor. Rutland was accepted by the English faculty until he met Traci a year ago at the pre-semester faculty orientation during which the president always welcomed the faculty to another academic year and discussed the new fiscal aspects. Since both were late for the orientation, they met outside of the auditorium doors and, smitten at once like two teenagers, decided to go to the cafeteria for coffee and skip the boring orientation. From that meeting on, they were inseparable; both agreed that something "just clicked" for them. The fact that they weren't in the same department was a plus for them; there could be no suspicion of collusion on department matters or possible accusation of early nepotism.

Coincidentally, both of their apartment leases expired in September; they decided to find a larger apartment and move in together.

Gerald looked at his watch. Twelve-fifteen. He couldn't wait to tell Marion about John of Parthenon Press and about Rutland's book. He wanted to tell her in person, not on the phone. He picked up his attaché case from the desk and, with long hurried steps, switched the lock and closed the door.

* * * * *

"Hello," Sarah said into the phone.

"Sarah, this is Marion Ritchey. How are you?"

"All right."

"I'm glad. I talked to Edward at Rex's dinner party and told him I'd like to visit with you. It's been a while. He said that would be fine."

"Of course it would, Marion. You know you're welcome any time and I'd love to see you. It gets a little lonely here with Edward away so much. He goes to every conference there is. Sometimes I think he just goes somewhere to get away from me."

"Oh, Sarah, I don't think that's true."

"Well, it seems that way to me."

"Hasn't the weather been glorious?"

"Perfect. Why don't you come out for lunch one day and we can sit outside? I'll have Lela do a Crab Louis for us with some home baked hard rolls."

"That sounds great. Which day is good for you?"

"Any day you wish."

"Well, I can have Gerald drive me out after his morning classes on Wednesday."

"He can come for lunch also. I haven't seen him in ages. Then he can tell me how his book is coming along."

"It's finished and off to a publisher."

"How wonderful. I wish the best for both of you."

"Thank you, Sarah. May I bring a nice Chardonnay to go with the crab?"

"Nothing. Just yourselves."

"How about dessert? You always liked my lemon cake."

"Now that you mention it. If that's not too much trouble...."

Marion laughed. "Good."

"I can taste the butter and lemon already."

"Then we'll see you on Wednesday, shortly after noon."

"Fine. I'm looking forward to it."

"See you."

* * * * *

Lizbeth Rostrand pulled up to the gate in her sleek black Jaguar sedan, pressed the opener, and the huge iron gate swung inward silently. She loved teaching, but she loved coming home to the peacefulness of her Spanish villa sprawled on five acres. The gate closed automatically behind her. She slid the car left and parked on the terra cotta-tiled courtyard near the four-tiered Mexican fountain.

She was fortunate to have found this hacienda five years ago when she first came to the valley. She had stayed at The Ranch for weeks while she toyed with the idea of renting or buying. Her family's life-style dictated owning, so she drove around looking for sites. Dozens of homes were hidden along intricate roads in the canyons, yet most homes had views from ultra grand 360-degree to straightforward outlooks on rolling hills. While searching the often hidden single-lane roads, she also learned about the circuitousness of them and the often treacherous heights leaping down the passenger side as she drove up them.

One afternoon she drove up a dirt road she had somehow missed during her other searches. She was not too far up the hill when she spied a "For Sale by Owner" sign stapled to the door of a huge barnlike wooden mailbox. She pulled into the driveway and halted at the speaker five feet from the gate. She buzzed. While she waited for a response, she admired the orange tile roof, the fountain bubbling happily in the afternoon sun, the huge years-old red and pink oleander bushes lining both sides of the crushed-stone drive.

A voice broke her intense observation. "Yes." It was said as if it was in answer to a question.

"I was driving by and saw your "For Sale" sign. When may I come by to see your place?"

"Right now if you wish."

"Fine."

There was a buzz and then the iron gate—designed in the shape of a huge split Spanish fan captured in a frame—swung inward. As she pulled close to the house, the massive carved mahogany front door slid slowly open. As if stepping out of the nineteenth century, a petite woman in full-length multi-petticoated black silk seemed to glide across the patio to greet Lizbeth. Her porcelain face, haloed by jet-black hair caught in a loose ponytail, was held by a silver buckle barrette.

She extended her multi-ringed hand.

"Consuelo Valencia," she said.

"Lizbeth Rostrand."

They shook hands gently but firmly; a cluster of various-width silver bracelets jangled loose from enormous ruffled sleeves.

Consuelo smiled; her teeth were pearls in her olive skin; her lips were naturally, softly red.

"Lovely courtyard," Lizbeth said.

"But you must come in and see the rest of the house. You cannot always tell from the outside what you might find inside."

Consuelo spoke the words without hesitancy—as if they were a good second language for her; there was the slight hint of an accent.

In the center of the entrance hall, a low colorful mosaic fountain gurgled; broad dark beams accented the white plaster ceiling. Typical Spanish *hacienda* but *grande*. The living room featured a hand-carved mahogany fireplace with a six-foot opening. On the mantel were silver candelabras and a huge silver urn. Behind the four-foot lacy andirons lay the remnants of the morning fire; weak orange and blue tongues slithered along the embers and licked the last of the charred wood.

Lizbeth followed Consuelo to the arched ten-foot windows which opened onto the inner courtyard with potted palms; islands of ferns; red, orange, and pink bougainvilleas on ten-foot trellises; pink and red camellias; gardenias; and a rainbow of impatiens around a 45-foot swimming pool with mural-tile dolphins playing on the bottom.

"This is breathtaking."

Consuelo smiled as she looked on the scene in the same appreciative way Lizbeth was seeing it.

"My husband and I had many beautiful years here."

Lizbeth did not respond. She waited.

"He died last year of leukemia."

"I'm sorry."

Consuelo crossed herself. "He suffered much." She paused as if she were seeing him suffer the agony all over again. Once more she crossed herself and then gently kissed the tips of her fingers as if they were her husband's dying lips. "I thought I could live here forever. Now I know that I can't. That's why I want to sell." She paused. "But not to just anyone." She looked directly into Lizbeth's eyes, a soft smile on her lips. "I don't want real estate agents bringing everyone in here. I am selective because this was a home of love and still is special to me." And then she said, "Let me show you the rest of the house."

A lavishly large dining room featured the same grand fireplace as the living room, but without the embers of a fire; a long highly polished ebony table reflected the three silver twelve-candle candelabrum on its surface; twenty high-backed tapestry-upholstered chairs surrounded it. The great kitchen had an open fireplace, two mahogany SubZero refrigerators, two six-burner Viking range tops, four ovens, a bank of stainless sinks set in gleaming black granite countertops, and a long black granite island above which gleaming cooking utensils dangled. Four bedrooms—again, all with fireplaces framed in handpainted Mexican tiles—and private baths with sunken marble tubs and dual-shower stalls.

"We entertained a great deal. But since he's dead, I haven't had anyone here. I just want to be alone with him and my memories."

Lizbeth knew this *hacienda* was for her.

"Your house is magnificent. I would like to buy it as furnished as possible."

Consuelo looked at her in astonishment. *"Por cierto."*

Lizbeth put out her hand; Consuelo took it, held it for a moment. Then she embraced Lizbeth in a motherly way—cheek to cheek.

"Come with me," Consuelo said.

They reentered the living room and Consuelo led her to the fire place. She took Lizbeth's hand and held it as she looked up at the urn, then to Lizbeth, then back to the urn.

"Now, will you tell my husband what you said?"

* * * * *

"Oh, Lizbeth, we're so happy for you," her mother said.

Her father was listening on an extension.

"Darling, just give me the name of your bank and your account number and I'll transfer money in the morning."

They had always shared their wealth with Lizbeth; she always had her own bank account when she lived at home. Now they saw to it that a generous deposit was made to her Wells Fargo account each month. There was nothing she could not afford.

Thereafter, the summer was spent at showrooms in San Francisco with the designer-owner of Furnishers West in Carmel.

* * * * *

Sheila answered on the fourth ring.

"Hi. Long time no see."

"Oh, hi."

She was caught off guard.

"What's up? What've you been doing? Haven't heard from you since July."

60

"Michael, that's not true."

"Well, it seems like it was that long ago."

"I've been with my family in Hawaii," she lied.

"Lucky you. How was it?"

"Great. We did different islands this time."

"Yeah. Which ones? Not that it would matter, since a poor guy like me from Seattle wouldn't know one from another unless I had a map in front of me, and then they'd just be names."

"Then why should I bother?"

"True."

"And stop feeling sorry for yourself."

He was quiet a moment.

"I'd sure like to see you."

"I'm tired, Michael."

"I bet I could perk you up."

She felt her heart beat a little faster.

"I don't think so."

"Let me try."

She shook her head as if to dispel the thought. She closed her eyes and said, "Michael, I think it's over."

"Funny, I don't think so."

She didn't answer.

"Are you thinking about what great times we had? Is that why you're not answering?"

"No, Michael, that's not it."

"Is there someone else?"

"Michael, if there's no time for you, how could I have time or energy for someone else?"

"You tell me."

He was beating her down. Her heart was thumping. *Could he hear it over the phone? Of course not.* But she was weakening. Of course, she had lied to Edward. As she lay in bed with him when he asked about Michael, she knew she was lying. *But why have a confrontation when none of it really mattered?* When she said she had tapered off and there was nothing, she meant that she had tapered off—meaning it was not as often with Michael. She felt herself grow warm and then hot as Michael said things into the phone. He mentioned a number of their wildly passionate actions and moments, but she didn't answer.

"I'll be there in twenty minutes," he said.

* * * * *

Michael had left Seattle, Washington, at eighteen, because he was tired of rain. He wanted sunshine. Where else but sunny California? When he told his dad about his decision, his father—understanding the free spirit of a youth because he had had the same drive when he was young—told him that he would never hold him back. They enjoyed a wonderful father-son relationship.

Michael's mother had died from uterine cancer four years ago, and he and his dad had batched it pretty well. Their diet did not consist of McDonald's hamburgers, Pizza Hut pizzas, and Kentucky Fried Chicken. They both cooked—but not gourmet: Meat, mashed potatoes, canned gravy and vegetables were their mainstays. They seemed to thrive and they helped each other to keep the house in order.

Michael's dad was a hearty individual—always finding something to laugh about. He was a fine mechanic with an excellent supervisory job at Seattle's largest Exxon station. In his spare time, he went salmon fishing. When he brought home salmon, he fileted them, grilled enough for the two of them, then froze the balance for later.

When Michael left, his dad gave him two thousand dollars to get started, and told him never to forget that he always has a home in Seattle and, that if he ever needed anything, to call.

So Michael bought a Greyhound bus ticket to San Francisco and stayed at the YMCA. Fog for days. Cold.

He bought another bus ticket to go south to Monterey. It was July and the fog was unusually heavy. He liked the area; it was clean and movie-set beautiful. When he went to lunch or dinner, he talked with the countermen or waitresses and asked about the sunshine. They told him that to get all the sunshine he wanted, he should investigate Carmel Valley.

He took a local bus from Monterey and found that the incredible demarcation line between cold and fog and blue sky and sun was about eight miles into the valley. Farther on, in the heart of the valley, he rambled in dazzling sunshine among buildings and streets of the one-story Western-like village. He knew this was where he wanted to live.

In his meanderings, he saw a hand-written "Help Wanted" sign in the Carmel Valley Market store window and went in to apply. Randy, the owner, hired him immediately; Michael told him that he had to get his things from Monterey and find a place to live; Randy told him about an apartment building not too far from the store, and he took his suggestion. It was furnished and in poor condition; however, for the time being, he would take it on a month-to-month basis which the landlord was more than happy to agree to; after a while, he could look for something else.

When he established himself in the apartment, cleaned it thoroughly, and signed for a post office box, he called his dad and gave him the whole scoop.

Ever conscious of a boy's needs, his dad said, "Michael, you'll need a car."

"I don't think so. Not right now."

"Michael, I'll send you a check and you buy yourself a nice used car. I want you to have it. Have a good mechanic look at it before you buy it."

The check arrived and he bought an '84 Ford Bronco II with a V6 engine which the local Beacon mechanic said was in great condition and a "damned good buy."

He had driven his dad's car and had a license; all he had to do was get a smog test, go to the Department of Motor Vehicles in Seaside to register, and apply for a California license.

He worked seven days at the market—from seven-thirty until three-thirty. One of his regular customers overheard him talking about his need for an apartment and she recommended a small house near the river; she gave him the name and address. Martha Perkins, the owner, was there; a cheerful elderly woman shoulder-bent with age— her unkempt, mottled grey hair in a tousled knot atop her head—who was going to live with her daughter because she was no longer able to take care of herself; however, she didn't want to sell her home—only rent it.

For him it was perfect—a little musty, but he could air it. She was renting it furnished. It had a small kitchen; a small bath with a non-turn-around-in shower; a living room with an aged bentwood rocker;

a patchwork-quilt-pattern sofa in front of a river-rock fireplace; and a bedroom with a double bed.

He rented it.

In Michael's presence, Martha called her daughter and asked when she could come to pick her up.

"Day after tomorrow? All right, I'll tell him. He's a nice young man. Bye."

The "Bye" was almost a trill.

Although it wasn't the end of the month, Michael couldn't bear to stay in his apartment a day longer than necessary. Midafternoon, two days later, Michael parked behind a red Taurus alongside the blackened irregular 2x2 wood post fence hugging the house and went in. The owner's daughter had just finished cleaning and had already packed her mother's belongings into suitcases and taken them to the car.

The daughter gathered up her cleaning materials and wished him happiness here. As she left, she stressed the fact that the rent was due *before* the first of every month and the address to which he should send it was on the sink drainboard.

That afternoon he unpacked and drove back to the store to buy everything he needed to stock the small refrigerator and the cupboards.

He had his own house; within two days, he had a phone.

Sometime later, he discovered Orchard Supply in Sand City and bought a dozen Airwicks to kill the mustiness in the house caused by the lack of sun, the density of the oak trees, and the nearness to the river. From talking with neighbors, he learned that all of the surrounding houses had the same problem and that there was nothing he could do about it; he would have to live with it.

Two months later, mounting expenses made him realize that he needed a job that paid better wages. He answered a Sunday *Herald* advertisement for a salad bar trainee at a wharf restaurant in Monterey. He called, was interviewed, and—probably because he was such a clean-cut young man—was notified by a phone call that he was hired. They asked him to come to the office to fill out forms and talk further with the chef.

Randy, the store owner, hated to see him leave, but said that he would never hold back an ambitious young man. He gave him a fatherly hug and pat on the shoulder and wished him the best.

Michael started to work at the restaurant on the following Monday.

He soon came to realize that, since Valley Villa College was near his home, he should take some courses toward a degree in computer science. That fall he registered and began classes.

During his early morning class sessions at the college, he met Sheila Mercer. Michael was young and handsome; she was attractive and hot.

That was how it all started.

Chapter 5

MARION DROVE GERALD TO THE COLLEGE for his morning classes and picked him up at twelve-fifteen in front of the Humanities Building. He sat in the passenger seat and leaned over to kiss her before he seat-belted himself.

"Did you bake a cake?" he asked.

"Now, Gerald, darling, what do you think? It's still warm. I have it in a cake safe in the trunk." She turned on the ignition, released the handbrake, slipped into drive.

"How were classes?"

"Good."

Marion, always the adoring listener, let him talk.

"These two classes are eager freshmen groups. They listen intently and try hard to apply everything I tell them. They're among some of the best groups I've ever had."

Marion looked at him, smiled, reached over and touched his knee. "Darling, you say that about all of your classes."

He patted her hand on his knee, tilted his head, and returned her smile. "Well, my Tuesday-Thursday classes are a bit slower, but they're trying."

Sarah and Edward's house was located near the mouth of the valley in a cul-de-sac off the Valley Road. It was a one-story ranch house among four others—different in design—of redwood and river rocks and glass expanses designed to provide scenic views rather than views of boring Valley Road traffic. The architect who designed it must have lived on or visited the site in all seasons and studied the morning sun's approach and the evening sun's demise before he designed it because the situation of the house and the glass exposures to nature were ideal. There was never the wrong intrusion of sunlight into the house at the wrong time of day, and the entire garden was planted according to the needs of the vegetation: shade, partial sun, full sun. California live oaks—more than a hundred years old—shaded the house from the blistering summer afternoon sun and kept the house ten-to fifteen-degrees cooler than the outdoor temperature.

Marion and Gerald turned into the parking area alongside the house; the driveway continued a hundred yards or more to the garage. He went to the trunk and took out the cake.

"Thanks, darling," she said.

They never failed to thank each other for anything, no matter how trite a thing one of them might do for the other. People often noticed this trait and marveled at the love which lay in those minor politenesses.

The entrance was a redwood Dutch door and the top was open.

"Hello. Sarah?" Marion called.

"Come in."

Sarah was seated in a wing chair near the fireplace, the ever-present crutches leaning beside her against the left wing. She was dressed in a green linen dress, V-cut into her bosom, a single strand of pearls at her throat.

Lela came out of the kitchen as they entered.

They exchanged pleasantries and Marion handed the cake to Lela.

"You can take it out of the cake safe and let it cool some more, Lela."

Lela nodded and began to remove the steamy plastic cover even before she got to the kitchen door.

"It's wonderful to have you here," Sarah said. "I don't have many visitors."

As a matter of fact, after the first few months, after the flowers died, after the fruit and candy were eaten, no one came or called. It was as if all who knew her had done their obligatory duty to send regrets and best wishes and then had forgotten her. *But really,* she often thought, *when I think about it, isn't that the way it always is and always has been? I've been guilty of that myself.*

Marion went to her, kissed her on the cheek, and said, "I'm sorry we haven't been to see you more often lately. It's been a crazy year for us."

"The year started out bad for me, too, and hasn't gotten any better," Sarah said.

The two high-backed upholstered wing chairs flanked the coffee table in front of the sofa where they sat. Sarah turned slightly to face them.

"What does the doctor have to say, Sarah?"

"Time, he says, just time and therapy."

She reached out and tenderly touched the crutches as if they were her two best friends.

Marion and Gerald looked at each other.

"Does he have any idea when you'll be able to walk again without crutches?"

"Probably never. He won't say. He just tells me to be patient and everything will be all right. Therapy has helped some and the pain has diminished. He wants me to go three times a week now. Tuesday, Thursday, and Saturday. Lela drives me. I bicycle slowly, very slowly, and walk stiff-leggedly no more than five miles an hour on the treadmill. That's almost like standing still. But, I suppose you could call that some progress."

Changing the subject, Sarah said, "Lela prepared lunch on the back patio. Shall we go out?"

She leaned on the arms of the chair to support her rise. As she reached for the crutches, Marion started to help her, but Gerald held her back.

Sarah caught the action and said, "I can do it, Marion. I've had to learn to do it myself. If I didn't, I'd be in this chair for days on end."

She gave a little nervous laugh as she lifted herself, put her hands in the crosspieces of the crutches and swung her legs around toward the kitchen.

They followed her out of the kitchen door to the patio.

Lela had set the round umbrella table with a cheerful yellow cloth, a bowl of yellow margaritas, and yellow napkins. Plates were already set with lump Dungeness crabmeat in crisp cups of Boston lettuce. After they sat, Lela poured a glistening Joullian Chardonnay. A serving boat of homemade pink Louis sauce was waiting to be passed. As Sarah promised, Lela had made hard rolls which were still warm; they were passed with melon-shaped balls of butter on crushed ice.

"Sarah, this is lovely," Marion said.

"Lela is a jewel. I don't know what I'd do without her."

They launched into their lunch.

Conversation was minimal.

When Lela removed the plates, Sarah said, "Gerald, did you go to the English conference in San Francisco?"

"No. I didn't know there was one."

Marion looked at Gerald.

"I was amazed at how early the conferences were starting. In mid-September already, just a few weeks after the semester started, Edward left on Wednesday afternoon and came back Sunday morning. It had something to do with Shakespeare."

"Well, that's not my field."

"Edward said that there are more meetings and conferences scheduled for this year than he can ever remember. Do you find it so, Gerald? How the classes will suffer. You certainly can't keep up with your syllabus if you go to all of them."

"Actually, Sarah, I never go to conferences or meetings. I just don't like to go away. I guess I'm just a stick-in-the-mud and hard to budge from my routine."

"Maybe that's good," Sarah said. "I wish Edward was more like you."

Lela served wedges of Marion's lemon cake and they ate without talking except for Sarah's sounds of appreciation for the dessert. No one wanted coffee.

A warm soft breeze started up and the red geraniums in urns waved their ruffled leaves. The pink-and-white petunias in redwood boxes at the edge of the deck jostled each other and their blossoms folded back on themselves.

"Marion told me you finished your book."

Meekly, Gerald smiled.

Marion reached over and touched his hand. "May I tell her, Gerald?"

Gerald nodded.

"John Stanton, the sales representative from Parthenon Press, has taken it back with him to New York and is personally delivering it to the fiction editor as a favor for Gerald. Isn't that great?"

"Oh, Gerald. I wish you everything good. You deserve it."

She crossed her fingers on both hands and held them up for him to see.

"Thank you."

"Oh," said Sarah, "how was Rex's dinner party?"

"Lovely," Marion said.

"Edward didn't say too much. I was asleep so I don't know what time he came home, but it must have been quite late because I read until twelve and then fell asleep with the light on. He must have gone to Lizbeth Rostrand's. He said she was having people to her house afterwards."

Neither Marion nor Gerald uttered a word. They knew that Lizbeth Rostrand never entertained faculty. She was a very private person. They gave each other a fleeting glance and Marion said, "We don't know. If so, we weren't invited. But, let me tell you, she was as stunning as ever."

"She has elegance, sophistication, and—evidently—family money and can afford to be," Sarah said without rancor or jealousy. "I think the amazing thing is that she doesn't display any sense of superiority or snobbishness. Edward said that she's a fine teacher and that the students adore her."

"That's true," Gerald said.

Marion changed the subject back to the party in answer to Sarah's question.

"Rex was a wonderful host as always. It was a beautiful evening. Oh, and Sarah, at his party, he promised to take us to Tarpy's for a celebration when Gerald's book was finished and gone. Which he did. Champagne and filet mignon. That was another memorable evening. He's a wonderful man and very supportive of his staff."

"I know. Edward was fortunate to be interviewed by him. Just by chance he had been to an English conference in November in San

71

John Bodnar

Francisco and several teachers were there from Valley Villa. He had delivered a talk on Shakespeare and they introduced him to Rex. That's the beginning of it all."

"I know," Marion said. "We were all fledglings together *here*, but we had all gotten our feet wet elsewhere."

"Marion," Gerald said, "I didn't hear that worst of all clichés! That's divorce material."

They had a good laugh.

"I needed that, Marion," Sarah said.

"I could have done *without* that, Marion," Gerald said.

Marion puckered her lips into the air. Gerald puckered back.

"So much has happened in our lives since we moved here from Omaha. You know, though, Marion, we had a wonderful life there. When we drove to Nebraska for Edward's first job, we were on Interstate Eighty and I said to Edward, 'My God! There's Oz!' I had never seen such an incredibly beautiful sight in my life. In the distance, on the horizon, the city rose straight up out of the flat land. And for the breadbasket of the nation, there was little growing in the parched fields at the end of that June."

Gerald looked at his watch. "Gosh, it's almost two-thirty. We should be going, Marion. I'm sure we've tired you, Sarah."

"Not at all. I usually rest in the afternoon, but this has been wonderful for me. Having company has relaxed me and I won't need to take a sleeping pill this afternoon."

Gerald and Marion smiled and stood. Marion said, "We've got to do this again soon."

"I hope so," Sarah said. "I get terribly lonely."

Driving home, they were silent. It wasn't until they were almost to their turnoff that Gerald said, "I wonder which conference Edward went to."

Marion turned and looked at him.

* * * * *

Gerald tore off the date on his desk calendar and thought, *My God, the first week of October is almost over.*

The phone rang.

Gerald picked up the handset.

"Gerald, it's Rutland. I just wanted to see if you were there. My author's copies arrived this morning and I promised you a copy as soon as they arrived. May I come over now?"

"Absolutely."

He restacked the exams he was correcting and began to put the scores in his roll book.

Rutland came in five minutes later, clutching the book with a full-color dust jacket of a young John Edgar Wideman against a montage of scenes from his books, but mainly his Pittsburgh Homewood trilogy. He handed it to Gerald.

"Great dust jacket, isn't it?"

"One of the best I've seen, Rutland. Berkeley always does a professional job. Nothing to be ashamed of. Will you sign it for me?"

"I already have. You don't think I'd give you an unsigned copy, do you?"

Gerald opened the book, read the inscription and smiled. After laying the book down, he walked around the desk, extended his hand, shook heartily, and punctuated it with a friendly hug and back pat.

"Thank you. That's a great honor and compliment."

"I know this is impromptu, but Traci and I would like you and Marion to have dinner with us this evening to celebrate the event. What do you say?"

"I think we'd love to, but let me call Marion to see if it's okay for me to accept. You know how women are...their hair and all?"

Rutland nodded and smiled as Gerald called home.

"As you heard, Marion would be delighted. And she said, 'Congratulations.'"

"How about seven?"

"Okay. And that's on Esplanade Drive? Right?"

"Right. Apartment 248."

* * * * *

Edward parked the car in the driveway rather than put it in the garage, because he was going to make a trip after dinner. *What would be his excuse?* He hadn't thought it out yet. As always, something would come to him at the last minute.

73

Until today, as he was locking his office door, he hadn't seen Sheila since mid-September except "for a drop-in" during his office hours which made him nervous. When she arrived, they closed the door, but even as he worried about student interruptions, there was something dangerously exciting about fooling around with her in the office. They never had sex on the desk, although she suggested it a couple of times. Today, however, as he turned around to leave, they were face to face *outside* of the locked office door.

"Hello, Professor Kendrick. I see I almost missed you. How are you?"

"Hello, Miss Mercer. Fine. How are you?

"Fine. I haven't seen you much this semester."

"I've been here. My office door is always open."

She looked up at him and gave a broad smile of insinuation. Under her breath, she said with a mischievous smile, "Not always."

Just then two of his colleagues came by and she turned to greet them.

Edward nodded to them. When they were out of earshot, Edward said, "How's tonight?"

"Sevenish?"

"I'll be there."

* * * * *

In the kitchen, Sarah stood at the sink rinsing lettuce, tearing it, and placing it in the spinner. Her crutches leaned against the drainboard beside her.

"Hello," Edward sang. When he was "up" for whatever reason, his greeting always had a little singsong ring to it.

"Hi, there, *you* sound happy."

She twisted herself around to look at him. He was a handsome man. Today he was wearing a tie with small white polka dots on a navy background and a Ralph Lauren white button down shirt with bold navy stripes under his double-breasted navy cashmere blazer with which he wore medium grey slacks.

Some people might call that outfit an academic cliché, but what else can a professor wear and look this classy?

She went warm inside.

He set his attaché case flat on the white tile island in the center of the kitchen and clicked it open.

"I have a little surprise for you. Close your eyes."

"Okay."

He stood beside her, his outstretched hand in front of her.

"Open," he said.

"Oh, Edward! A new Anne Tyler! I didn't know she had one."

"*A Patchwork Planet,*" he said, "and the *Times* review is great. By the way, I didn't know her husband died, did you? She's dedicated it to his loving memory. From the little I've read about them, they were a devoted couple. They've always avoided publicity and interference into their personal lives."

Sarah leaned against the sink and dried her hands with paper towels which she wrenched from the rack on the wall. She took the book and read the blurb on the dust jacket.

"Thank you, Edward."

She kissed his lips gently.

He didn't add any pressure to the kiss. He merely took her arms in his hands, smiled, closed his eyes, and nodded.

"You're welcome," he said as he moved away from her.

"I'll start it tonight after dinner."

"I'm glad I bought it, because I have to go back to the college after dinner. I promised George Short I'd take his class tonight because he had to be in San Jose today for a late afternoon guest lecture and wouldn't be able to make it back in time for his eight o'clock."

"I see. Then we'll eat about six. Okay?"

"Good."

When he went back to his room to shower, she smiled as she watched him swagger down the hall, swinging his attaché case, and humming.

* * * * *

As he drove down the Valley Road past Scarlett Road, he thought he saw Marion and Gerald Ritchey in the oncoming traffic headed toward mid-valley. There was no indication that they saw him, but if, as an afterthought, they realized it was him, at least they would think he was headed toward the college. They lived in a rented house just off Los Tulares and if they had seen him beyond The Running Iron making a right turn on Robles del Rio, they would have cause to question his being there.

Edward was pleased about his quick-thinking ruse to get away for the evening. He elaborated from habit, when Sarah asked, that the class was an hour-and-a-half and that there was one office hour afterward and that, by the time he got home, it would be after eleven. He told her to go to bed and not to wait up. She said she would. He kissed her cheek when he left. She thanked him again for the Anne Tyler and told him she loved him. He did not say, in return, that he loved her.

This, then, should be a sensational evening.

The last time they had spent any *really meaningful* time together was the long mid-September weekend in San Francisco when she had cut her Thursday and Friday classes because they both wanted, finally, to be together for more than a few stolen hours. He had bought her a jade bracelet at Gump's; at an elegant jewelry shop in Ghirardelli Square, she had bought him a Baccarat crystal satyr for his desk, which she said symbolized their heated relationship and which she wanted never to end now that she found the man who satisfied her well and often. They had had wonderful days: eating at intimate out-of-the-way French restaurants; seeing the *real* Chinatown and eating at local Grant Avenue restaurants where the food was deliciously authentic and served in unpretentious surroundings—not the kind of Chinese cuisine that Dakotans expected to be served in a luxuriously gold-and-black ambiance with green ceramic Foo Dogs and green-and-gold dragons. He took her to Ferlinghetti's *City Lights* bookstore at the end of Grant Avenue, which wound up on famous North Beach, hoping that Ferlinghetti would be there. He told her about Kerouac and Ginsberg, and the hippy commune movement of North Beach—of which she had no knowledge, but which she said she would have joined had she been around at the time. He bought her a copy of *A Coney Island of the Mind*—Ferlinghetti's most famous work—and promised her that they would read it in bed together and that he would explain some of the masterpieces to her. They laughingly hopped onto cable cars; he pointed out Danielle Steele's white mansion on the corner as they rode by; they looked down the crookedest street in the world; they had Irish coffees in the Buena Vista at the end of the Powell Street Cable Car line. She got a great kick out of the way everyone lined up at the bar, the bartender pouring Irish whiskey into a lineup of glass mugs at the head of the bar, then filling the mugs with steaming coffee, and finally topping them with globs of Irish whiskey whipped cream before he sent them careening down the gleaming bar for the recipients to catch. There were great camaraderie and laughter—and repeat orders—especially at Happy Hour. They ate clam chowder out of sourdough bread bowls among the milling crowds on Fisherman's Wharf.

* * * * *

Suddenly he was there. Without realizing it, he was turning into the driveway. The living room light was on; there was only the ghost of a light in the kitchen window overlooking the parking area.

He took the stairs two at a time like a teenager; without knocking, he burst into the room. Sheila was reading on the sofa, her exposed legs curled under her. Measuredly, she set her book on the end table and rose. He hungrily enveloped her mouth with his. When they finally and reluctantly separated, she said, "It's been too long."

"I know."

He ran his hands over her back and sides; he moved his mouth to her breasts. She sighed heavily, took his hand, and led him into the bedroom. She peeled off his coat as he undid his tie. Quickly and deftly, she unbuttoned his shirt and tore it out of his trousers. He opened her robe and she let it drop to the floor. She stood naked before him. He kissed her hungrily as she unzipped his trousers which fell to the floor; he stepped out of them. His hands cupped her buttocks and he pulled her against his taut erection. She slipped his shorts down and held his erection in her hand. Their lips never parted. They sat on the bed and hurriedly finished undressing; she, her slippers; he, his shorts, shoes, and socks. They rolled into the middle of the bed and she mounted him. His hands worked her breasts and his thumbs rubbed her erect nipples as she rode him.

"Harder!" he said.

* * * * *

77

Marion and Gerald arrived on time. Rutland opened the door and greeted them; Traci called greetings from the kitchen and said she'd be right in.

They went into the comfortably monochromatically-furnished Danish living room; everything was ultra-modern teak and rosewood. The sofa was a teak platform with a beige thick-textured padded seat and a matching padded cushion back. The side chairs were sleek Danish teak, their legs slanted proportionately.

Rutland offered them a drink, and they asked for white wine. He had glasses for wine—white or red—and champagne flutes ready on the rosewood bar. He poured, gave them a mosaic cloth napkin, poured himself one and called, "Honey, come and have a toast with us."

"Be right there love. Don't drink without me," Traci called.

He poured red wine and handed it to her as she came in.

"Here's to success and happiness," Marion said.

They clinked their glasses and drank.

"What was it Elaine Stritch sang in that musical? 'I'll drink to that!'" Rutland said as he sat in one of the side chairs.

"I don't know which musical it was, but I like the line," Gerald said. "So how does it feel to have your name on something in print?"

"Only God and I know," Rutland said.

They all chuckled.

"You'll find out," Rutland said.

"I pray it happens. But you know the perversity of publishers and the reading whims of the public. Out of curiosity, I bought a little book the other day at Borders and the whole thing was a cliché—from title to story. And the errors in it—grammatical and structural as well as authorial about things which never occurred in the book—were incredible. As I read, I made a list and ended up with ten double-spaced legal-size pages. I was going to send them to the publisher and a copy to the author. But who am I to argue when something is on the *New York Times* bestseller list for thirty weeks at twenty-four dollars? Besides, it would take a whole morning to draft a letter and point out the errors. I guess it's my fault for buying it in the first place. I just wanted to see what the public was buying. If this is a sample, my book will die before it's born."

Gerald sipped his wine.

"It *is* amazing that we have to write for a specific audience in order to survive as writers. The days are gone when literacy was the hallmark for reading."

"No one wants to think," Gerald said.

"Or knows *how*?" Rutland said. "I find it in my lit classes also. The students want to be hand-fed. They want the answers without the task. TV, lazy teachers, and unconcerned parents have done that. The only time parents are concerned is when the student is failing. And then they blame it on the teacher. I pity the *good* high school teacher. Thank God we're spared—by law—talking to parents. Can you imagine what a farce that would be? I mean, when they're in college, they're adults and should be treated as such. They've got to assume responsibility for what they do or do not achieve."

"Getting back to books. Have you seen what's on the *Times* best-seller list? Mysteries, murder stories, suspense, horror. They finally created a separate list for Harry Potter after he knocked everyone off for more than a year. The only touches of romanticism have been *Madison County* and *Message in a Bottle*, and they are far from being great pieces of literature. But at least there's still a market for an occasional romance without violence."

"But they sold millions of copies and were made into movies. So, who are we to criticize? Silly-assed professors who don't earn millions."

"Enough. Why is it that academicians always talk shop or books when they're together?"

"If they didn't, Gerald, they wouldn't be good teachers or professors," Marion said.

They all laughed.

"So, what's new on the romance front?" Gerald asked.

Traci reached over and took Rutland's hand.

"In June. After the semester is finished, we'll tie the knot and take off for Europe for a month at least. Maybe longer."

"That's wonderful. I'm so happy for you."

Rutland and Traci looked at each other, then Rutland said, "We're happy *you* are, but there's bad blood among some others—in both Traci's department and in ours."

"This is the twentieth century!" Marion said.

"And California, one of the most laid-back states in the Union."

"This is not a university in San Francisco or Los Angeles," Traci reminded them.

"I simply can't believe it." Gerald shook his head.

"Lots of small town minds. What's bothersome is that these are our educated colleagues. The native Californians who live here treat us without bias or question."

"Have you talked to the department heads or the Deans about this?" Gerald inquired.

"No."

"There must be something they can do."

"Short of what? The American Association of University Professors? Come on, Gerald, neither the college nor the AAUP would become involved. It has nothing to do with the college or its policies. It's all personal. Maybe the NAACP, but I don't want that kind of publicity for us or the college."

Gerald thought for a moment.

"I don't blame you. I wouldn't either."

"Have you talked to Jesse?" Marion asked. "As department chair, he might be able to do something."

"Among us, I don't find him very empathic about anything."

"But it's all so unfair," Marion said.

"Sometimes life is," Gerald answered.

Dinner was a delicious beef stroganoff—October was the perfect time for it—cubes of filet, sour cream, white wine, and sautéed mushrooms served with wild rice and spiced crab apples, peaches, and pears. Traci was a purist, Marion thought. The nonsense of putting tomato sauce in a Russian dish was asinine. A choice of fine Meridian Chardonnay or Merlot from Paso Robles accompanied it. Traci had made a grapefruit pie which was light and complementary. Miniature marshmallows melted in grapefruit juice with a touch of sugar, whipped cream, and grapefruit segments.

After dinner, when Traci and Rutland had cleared the table and they sat finishing a second bottle of wine, Gerald said, "Rutland, I want to thank you again for the beautiful inscription in your book."

He turned to Marion.

"You haven't seen it yet."

"What did he say?"

Gerald was almost tearful; he couldn't look at any of them.

"He wrote: 'To the finest person I know who also happens to be the best and the most loved and respected teacher on campus.'"

Marion said, "How beautiful, and how true."

She reached over and clasped her hand over Gerald's.

They finished the wine and said their goodnights; it was close to ten-thirty.

"Thank you for a beautiful evening and for letting us share this special occasion with you."

"Gerald, there's no one we would want to share it with but you and Marion?'" Rutland said.

* * * * *

Lizbeth arrived early at The Ranch Clubhouse. The final Friday afternoon in October was crisp, sparkling—almost like a Maine one: Missing were the semi-nude elm, oak, and maple trees and the lakes of crimson and gold leaves splashing underfoot. Such a vibrant day enticed golfers to an early lunch and game; there were only a few parking spaces; she parked on the lower level. Inside the clubhouse, she looked at some of the golf gear before she went to the hostess and was ushered to her reserved table by the window overlooking the expanse of active green.

After two weeks of separation for one unforeseen circumstance or another with which she had to contend, she and Gillian were having lunch, playing eighteen holes, and spending the weekend together. Lizbeth's reserve was broken; she was unnerved from longing and anticipation, no matter how many times she told herself that she must accept from Gillian whatever free time she was given and when.

The eager young waiter removed the other two place settings and, at her request, promptly brought her a glass of Chardonnay.

She perused the menu; momentarily, nothing appealed to her. She hadn't much of an appetite lately and she knew why.

She looked at her watch. Twelve-fifteen. She knew she was early, but—after weeks apart—she thought that Gillian might be also. No need to think negative thoughts. Positive is the answer.

The problem was that she longed for Gillian to live with her. Now that she had met someone, Lizbeth wanted a total live-in relationship.

81

She didn't want an occasional evening or weekend; she felt that their relationship could not thrive if that was the way it continued. They both were old enough....

But that wasn't the point; there were matters and conditions to consider which Lizbeth had to acknowledge and which had nothing to do with their affection for each other. It was all so frustrating. Lizbeth had never been in such a position as Gillian, so the conditions taxed her patience. She worried that she would become possessive and lose Gillian, that they might end up bickering and thus damage their relationship. *All could be so simple, but nothing ever is. So many ways to look at this. What comes too easily is not always as appreciated as something that comes with a struggle against odds.*

Gillian told her that she didn't think it was a good idea for her to live with Lizbeth. What if someone should find out that she had another woman living with her? How could they find out? Lizbeth told her that not only was she a very private person, but also that her colleagues were as well. What if someone just happened to drop by? She told her that no one would dare or even think to do such a thing. That no one she knew did that sort of thing. It just isn't done. Period. We respect each other's privacy.

Gillian had never invited Lizbeth to her home. That didn't matter. Lizbeth preferred things as they were; they had all the privacy they needed, and Lizbeth savored Gillian's wide-eyed enthusiasm about everything.

Over the rim of the glass, as she sipped her wine, she saw Gillian coming into the room. A broad smile on her face, a yellow scarf tied around her head—only a feathery tuft of chestnut hair escaped from it and lay on her tanned forehead. Her shorts and sleeveless yellow blouse intensified the density of her tan.

"I'm on time, thank God. I thought I'd be late. Traffic on Route One was backed up almost to the Del Monte turnoff. A truck stalled. The motor just died, and two cars plowed into it. It didn't look as if anyone was hurt."

"You're all right. That's what counts."

"Yes, thank God."

Then, "It's good to see you. And it's a perfect day for golf."

Gillian sat and the waiter—at her elbow immediately—spread her napkin across her lap. She thanked him and ordered the same as Lizbeth; in a few minutes, she was having her first sip of Chardonnay.

"You look ravishing as always," Gillian said.

"So do you. Seeing you enter the room, I had to catch my breath for a moment."

Gillian lowered her eyes shyly, let a smile cross her lips, reached across the table, and fleetingly touched Lizbeth's hand. Facets of pale purple fire glistened in the huge amethyst on her ring finger.

Lizbeth wanted to kiss it and feel the body heat from it warm her lips.

"What are our plans for the weekend?"

"Golf. And you, I hope. It's been too long," Gillian said.

"How about if we skip golf today and just lie by the pool and swim. Sun. Nude. And make love on one chaise lounge. Nude."

They laughed.

"I don't really want to share you—even on the golf course—this weekend."

They looked into each other's eyes, neglecting the fact that they were in public.

The waiter was at their side. "Excuse me, are you ready to order?"

They broke eye contact.

"Give us a few moments," Lizbeth said as she picked up her menu; Gillian let hers lay flat in front of her.

"I'll have the same as you," she said.

Lizbeth smiled warmly, slipped her hand across the table, then withdrew it in an incompleted gesture of affection.

The waiter returned when he saw her close the menu; Lizbeth looked up at him.

"Two Crab and Avocado Benedicts and two more Chardonnays, please."

"Yes, ma'am. Thank you." He repeated the order as he wrote it and seemed to scoop up the menus.

"While we're discussing plans," Lizbeth said, "We've never discussed Thanksgiving which is not too far away."

"Won't you be spending it with your mother and father?"

"Not if I can be with you."

83

"Oh, I'll be spending that week pretty much at home. My uncles and aunts—four of them—will be coming. They spend every Thanksgiving with us. I guess that's the only tradition we have left."

Looking directly into Gillian's eyes, Lizbeth asked rather pointedly, but with a dull sharpness: "Well, how *does* our time together look for these next weeks?"

"I'll see you every chance I have, Lizbeth, you know that."

"But I want more. This separation is tearing me down."

The waiter took away their empty glasses and set their fresh drinks before them; they thanked him.

Before she spoke again, Gillian lifted her glass in a toast. Lizbeth did likewise. They sipped; the cool wine came at a warm moment in their conversation.

Gillian set down her glass. "But you'll be busy, too, with your classes and other work. Not like me. All my time is nothing but bits and pieces, here and there."

"And all I get are the *other* bits and pieces here and there."

"Oh, Lizbeth, that's not fair. I'm seeing you every moment I can."

"I'm sorry. Well, perhaps I should go East for Thanksgiving. Yet, I'll be going back to Kennebunk for Christmas less than a month later."

"Have you decided on a date yet?"

"No."

They sat silently observing the tables around them.

"What can I give you for Christmas?"

"Nothing," Gillian said. "Just yourself. Anything else would be too hard to explain."

"It seems that I am, too."

Gillian looked questioningly at her.

"I mean, I'm hard to explain, too. Have you mentioned me to your parents?"

"Of course. But not in terms of our relationship. As a golfer."

"I see."

"And you? Have you told yours?"

"Not yet, but I will when the time is right."

"What do you mean by that?"

"When we're together."

"What do you think will be their reaction?"

84

"No problem. I think they already have a feeling about my life style, but have never verbalized it."

"Oh?

The waiter brought their meals.

"*Bon appétit*," he said.

* * * * *

Gerald was sitting at his desk working with a student on the first draft of a research paper due after Thanksgiving break in three weeks, when the college mail clerk delivered a FedEx box. Gerald looked up, saw the white box with the blue and red letters and his heart sank. It was the thickness of two reams of paper. The clerk approached him hesitantly—out of respect not to interrupt him—and he indicated that she should lay it on the corner of his desk. He smiled gratefully and she left.

During the entire discussion of the paper, Gerald's mind kept slipping to the delivery; occasionally his eyes wandered to the box, then returned quickly to the important work at hand: the student's writing.

After a half hour of paragraph-by-paragraph, page-by-page analysis of theme and structure, the student left—happy to be on the right track with the development of his research paper on Golding's *Lord of the Flies*.

Gerald sat for what seemed an hour, but which was only minutes, looking at the box on his desk, the pit of his stomach heavy with rejection and the desire to throw up.

Finding a single-edge razor blade in the inset of his center desk drawer, he slashed the box and withdrew the manuscript: It was rubberbanded with a cover letter.

Dear Professor Ritchey:

Thank you for letting John Stanton bring us your manuscript before anyone else had a chance to read it.

As you know, the market is flooded with fiction manuscripts by thousands of hopefuls, and we must think in terms of sales, because the cost of production for a mass market book is astronomical.

We read your manuscript with interest; we find the work real and plausible, but the length would not be marketable for us. The consumer cost would be almost unthinkable for a first work of fiction; for someone like Clancy, Uris, Koontz, or Gresham, the length would be no problem, because the sales would be predictable.

To cut several hundred pages would be a monumental rewrite task. However, should you decide to revise the work to a more acceptable length—keeping the theme intact, of course—I would appreciate your submitting it to us for another read. You could address it to me personally.

If you prefer not to revise, I wish you success in marketing your work with another house.

Sincerely,

Beth Wilson

Beth Wilson
Fiction Editor

He got up, closed his office door, returned to his desk, leaned back in his chair, and held the letter on his knee. He sat staring into space; his mind was blank. It wasn't until he felt a hot tear scald a trail down his cheek that he realized he was alive.

If you could call a rejection nice, *then it was a* nice *rejection letter,* he thought. *What now? Who now? I'm not revising it. It's the work I want it to be and the length I think it needs to be. But I've got to send it off again immediately since all of the reps have been here and won't be back until the middle of January. This is the first week of November. That's two months away and two months lost. I must send it again—and now.*

In his mind's eye, he ran through the reps who had offered to do what John Stanton had done. *Bill Slater at Carpenter.* He took his engagement book from the top drawer of his desk. In the front was the list of publishers and their representatives. He sat for a minute to collect himself and to think about what he would say.

He looked at his watch.

One o'clock.

Four on the East Coast.

Bill should be there, unless he left early.

Gerald dialed New York. The usual recording with a series of options ran for a minute. When the recording finally said that he should dial the extension of the person if he knew it, he dialed 7520. After four rings, Bill answered.

"Bill? Gerald Ritchey at Valley Villa in Carmel Valley. How are you?"

"Great. Good to hear from you. What can I do for you?"

"Well, you remember you offered to take my book to your fiction editor when it was ready?"

"Yes."

"Well, I'm ready."

"Good. Ship it to me and I'll get it to her ASAP."

"Thanks. I'll FedEx it. You'll have it tomorrow."

"I'll look for it."

What would he tell Marion? Nothing. He couldn't tell her anything. He never lied to her. This wasn't a lie, just an omission. Why should he have her concern herself? This was his project—even though they shared everything—and he should deal with it. Of course, she would be upset that he hadn't told her; after all, she was his soul mate and confidante for years throughout the entire creative process; besides, they always shared everything—good and bad. When I have good news, I'll tell her. But what if she asks me questions? What if she says, 'Have you heard anything about the book?' How will I answer? How can I not answer?

At his computer, he drafted a quick cover letter to Bill Slater, picked up the manuscript, and went to the Valley Business Service to prepare it for FedEx pick up. He'd send it "Next Day Delivery"; it would be in New York before ten a.m. tomorrow.

Chapter 6

AFTER THANKSGIVING BREAK, the semester always took on one of two aspects for the students; panic or a sigh of relief. Final examination dates were published in the student newspaper, and research papers were due.

After finals were taken, after corrected research papers were returned, grades were determined and submitted to the registrar's office by the second week of December.

While many students had part-time Christmas employment at Macy's or Mervyn's in the Del Monte Shopping Center in order to have money for presents, many others asked for full-time work after the semester officially closed. They could always expect to work through January fifth because of returns and inventory; those who found that they had some extra money after Christmas drove down to Laguna Beach or went off to one of the Hawaiian Islands—usually Oahu, because of its accessibility, great clubs, sunny beaches, string bikinis, hunky guys, and outrigger hotels.

Sheila stopped by Edward's office after her last final.

"I wanted to wish you a Merry Christmas," she said.

She was braless—her full round nipples strained against the beige silk blouse—and she was smoothly, underpantlessly poured into her thigh-high beige skirt.

Her auburn hair was soft and fluffed into fullness; her mouth sensual and painted with a metallic beige lipstick.

He was roused; he left his desk, went to his office door and closed it.

When he turned around, she was facing him. He enfolded her in his arms. She mashed herself against him, her nipples hardening from the heat and pressure of his chest.

"I'll miss you," he said when they finally parted enough to look at each other.

Their bodies were still pressed into each other. He kissed her *Passion*-sprayed hair near her ear and she shivered. He pushed his erection against her and she sighed deeply.

"Me, too," she said.

"Can I call you somehow?"

"We're leaving for Maui on the twentieth and won't be back until the tenth of January."

He groaned into her hair.

"I'll call you as soon as I get back. Will you miss me while I'm gone?"

She kissed his cheek.

He talked into her hair.

"Right now, I don't want to think about it."

She moved her arm from his waist and slid it between them.

"Oh, God," she sighed.

He bent his head down and breathed hotly into her blouse, careful not to moisten the silk with his breath. He undid several of the silk-covered buttons and opened her blouse enough for his mouth to envelop the nipple and soft white flesh of her breast.

"We have great sex, don't we?"

Her neck was strained as high as a swan's while he busied himself at her breast.

His answer was a deep moan.

"We'd better stop," she said, "or we'll have to finish on the desk, and we don't want to break the satyr I gave you."

"Merry Christmas," he said as he drew her taut nipple between his lips and wetly teased it with his tongue. He blew on it then to dry it before he rebuttoned the blouse.

"God," she said, "that's what's so different about mature men. They know what to do."

She kissed his dark, wavy hair; it smelled sexily clean.

When he returned to her lips, he crushed her open mouth—his tongue deep inside; her mouth was hungrily receptive.

Breathing heavily, they separated, their arms at their sides, their heads bowed.

"I'd better go."

"I think so, yet I don't want you to."

She held his face in her hands and kissed him softly on the lips.

"I'll call as soon as I get back," she said.

She turned, walked to the door, opened it, and didn't look back before she closed it behind her.

When he went to the door and looked in the direction she had gone, he saw no one. He left the door standing open and sat at his desk, looking into the hallway and seeing nothing.

* * * * *

Lizbeth was correcting finals, but without much progress. Her mind kept wandering to Gillian and their relationship.

Lizbeth did not go to Kennebunk for Thanksgiving; instead, she drove up to San Francisco on Wednesday evening and returned Saturday afternoon. She stayed at the Mark Hopkins, had leisurely morning room service, Thanksgiving dinner on the wharf, late evening drinks at the hotel, and then shared the infectious frenzy of holiday shoppers at Neiman's. At the designer shops such as Versace, Gucci, and Tiffany where she purchased a few new accessories, the pace was more sedate and the attention more personal. She saw a number of things at I. Magnin that she would like to have bought for Gillian, but the admonition that "she wouldn't be able to explain things away," prevented Lizbeth from doing anything more than looking at "things" and wishing.

The first weekend in December was the last time that they were together because Lizbeth was busy with giving and correcting finals, and, Gillian, because of the holidays, would be working overtime at Macy's in the Credit Department. During the week, she and Gillian talked on the phone as often as Gillian could call. When Gillian called Lizbeth at the college and Lizbeth could not speak freely, the one-sided conversation left them frustrated. After a call at home, Lizbeth wandered idly and aimlessly through the house, worthless for the balance of the day. Frequently, she would go to bed—like a child—and force herself to sleep in order to clear her mind of her desire to be with Gillian.

The phone rang.

Lifting the receiver, she said, "Professor Rostrand."

When she heard the voice, she ran her hand through her hair and leaned back in the chair.

"Yes, Rex, what a pleasure. And why so formal? How are you?"

"Good, thanks. What are your plans for the holidays?" Rex asked.

"I'm leaving on the sixteenth to go back to a winter Christmas in Maine with my family. Some skiing, hot toddies, fireplaces, the whole northeastern postcard fairy tale."

She laughed and he picked up on it.

"Since you're not leaving until the sixteenth, I wonder if you would accompany me to the AIDS Benefit on the tenth at the Doubletree in Monterey. It's an annual affair and has become one of the *big* events of the holiday season. I've gone for the past five years—always alone—but this time I'd like to have someone with me. I always go black tie, but we can go casual if you like. The chefs from at least six major restaurants in the area contribute hors d'oeuvres and a course—providing food, sous chefs, and kitchen help. Major vineyards in California—even vineyards as far away as Australia—contribute everything from champagne with the hors d'oeuvres to a different wine for each course."

"You sound like a running advertisement for a good cause."

He laughed.

"I'd be delighted, Rex. How nice of you to think of me."

If you only knew how often lately I think of you.

"I won't answer the obvious," he said. "It starts at seven. I'll pick you up. What's your address?"

She hesitated a second and then said, "Oh, Rex, that would be inconvenient. Why don't I meet you at the Doubletree?"

92

He was nonplussed.
He cleared his throat.
"It's no problem."
Although he couldn't understand, he detected a resistance.
"Okay," he said. "I'm happy just to have you join me."
"And I'm happy and flattered that you asked me."
"See you at seven at the Doubletree. I'll be wearing a black tie."
She laughed into the phone.
"You'll be the best looking black tie in sight."
"And you'll be the most stunning champagne blonde at the Doubletree."

* * * * *

Rex leaned back in his chair. Lizbeth was everything any man could possibly want.

He had not thought about marriage or dating since the pain of his divorce from Lora whom he married when they had completed undergraduate school at the University of Pittsburgh. She did not go on for her master's; instead, she taught math at nearby Schenley High School, while he continued to work on his master's degree. They never thought that the pressures of work on another degree would separate them as it had so many of their academic friends. Nights spent reading, writing papers, or doing research at the Carnegie Library in Oakland until it closed took its predictable toll on their relationship. Lora taught, corrected papers, cooked. They were both too tired to make love at the end of the day. Weekends were spent doing things they couldn't do during the workweek: planning meals, shopping, doing the laundry, ironing, cleaning. Lora had lesson plans to prepare for the week, homework to correct, tests to devise. Rex took his mentor's classes on occasion. He had to submit his thesis proposal and outline for approval and had to work on research for it as well as read and study for his classes and the classes he occasionally taught.

One weekend after Rex had finished his class work and was working full time on his thesis, Lora broached the subject of separation after Rex received his master's. There was no animosity in her declaration.

"Rex," she said. "You know I love you and I know you love me."

She was holding her wine glass in both hands in front of her mouth as she spoke; Rex had just finished wiping his mouth with his napkin and had picked up his wine glass. He held it in midair for a second and then set it down in front of his placemat.

"There has never been any doubt in my mind concerning our love for each other."

Lora didn't speak. She swirled the Merlot in her glass.

"Is there something you're trying to tell me? Have I done something wrong?"

Lora put down her glass and reached over to cover Rex's hand resting on the table.

"No, Rex."

"Then what...?"

"We haven't exactly had much of a marriage...."

Rex was silent.

Waiting.

Lora squeezed his hand. She was not looking at him, but down at their hands.

"Look at me," Rex said.

Lora looked into his eyes. "I never thought this could be true for us. And I never believed some of our friends when they told us to beware of the other degrees. But, it's true. We don't share any time together. I'm not blame-placing. You're working hard on your M.A. and I'm teaching with all the extras attached to it. Sometimes we don't even see one another at dinner. You're either researching or teaching a class for someone."

Rex took his eyes from hers. He removed his hand and sipped his wine. He stared at his wine glass after he set it down.

Lora reached across the table, but his hand was not within reach and he didn't meet hers with his. Rex stared down at it as it lay upturned and cupped on the table between them.

"I've been thinking. I know you want to work on your Ph.D. You won't want to get it here where you'll have your other two degrees. And I want you to get your Ph.D. But," she hesitated, "I can't leave my job so soon."

She had been looking at the top of his head as she spoke; now he looked up and met her eyes.

"What are you suggesting?"

"I don't want a divorce. I think, when you have your master's, that we should separate while you work on your doctorate. Then, when that's finished, we can make a decision."

"Lora, I don't want to lose you."

"I don't want to lose you either, but I think it would be best."

After a pause, she asked, "Have you decided where you'll work on your Ph.D.?"

"While I work on it at the University of Maryland, I have an offer to teach at a large two-year college nearby."

Lora said nothing.

Rex felt a tension rise in that space of time. "I didn't mention it to you, because I haven't decided yet to accept."

"Well, now you know I wouldn't hold you back."

She rose and went to him.

He stood and they embraced.

They were too emotionally distraught to seal the pact with anything other than a gentle cheek-to-cheek hug with eyes closed.

* * * * *

Rutland was going home with Traci to Hays, Kansas, for Christmas to meet her family for the first time. He wasn't quite sure how the heartland would take to him, but they loved each other and whether or not "they took to him" didn't matter to either of them. Traci was quite willing to give up everyone for him—her family and relatives, friends, whoever. Her spunk was one of the wonderful qualities he loved about her. As a true blond bombshell, she said, "I don't take shit from anyone. I don't have to!" When she said that or anything else she believed in, her little nose twitched in anger. It made Rutland chuckle. When he did, she broke up and kissed him, then punctuated the kiss with, "And I mean it!"

They were flying to Wichita, renting a car, and then driving on to Hays. As she said, "We have a car—like Bonnie and Clyde—to make our getaway, if there are any problems. Okay?"

Another punctuational kiss, followed this time by her ritual: she licked his forehead, curled a wisp of his hair, then plastered it into a "C" on his forehead with the flat of her hand.

95

* * * * *

"Hi, doll. How are you?"

"Fine. You?"

"Be better if I could see you over the holidays."

"Michael, I'm going to Hawaii with my family."

"Leaving tonight?"

"Of course not."

"So, how about it?"

She played the game.

"What?"

"Come on. You know what. What you like."

"Michael, I'm...."

"Don't give me that tired bullshit."

"Michael, I just have tons of stuff to do to get ready to go."

"Come on. You know how I feel about you. I don't want to, but I'll make it quick. You know I don't waste time."

"No."

"You know I don't take "no" for an answer, 'specially from you."

She changed the subject.

"How'd your finals go?"

"Would've been better if I didn't have you on my mind. My hard-on got in the way of my thinking processes."

She couldn't help laughing.

"You liked that, huh?"

"It was funny."

"But it's not. You never had one."

She laughed again.

"How about it? I don't know what I'll do if you don't see me."

"Take a cold shower."

"That won't help."

"Take two."

"Who is he?" Michael asked.

"Santa Claus."

"Yeah. And I'm the Easter Bunny."

He laughed.

"Pretty good characterization, huh?"

"Michael, have a good Christmas. I'll see you when I get back."

"Lot of catching up to do."

"I don't think so."

"We'll see. Have a good time on the island you're going to."

"Maui."

"Yeah."

He hung up.

* * * * *

When Rex stepped off the elevator into the lobby at The Doubletree Hotel, he was smitten by Lizbeth's glowing elegance. She wore a beige three-quarter length shawl which fell in folds and uneven spears around her flowing gown. She stood under one of the ceiling floodlights in front of a huge gold baroque mirror above a matching table. At either end of the table were massive urns of exotic flowers.

Gowned and freshly-coifed volunteers sat at a table just outside the banquet room, checking names off their lists as the guests presented their tickets.

Lizbeth didn't see him approach from the side until he was standing in front of her.

"Mirror, mirror, on the wall, who is the fairest one of all?"

She turned.

"The mirror tells me that you are as beautiful from the back as you are from the front. Good evening."

She turned and smiled at him.

"I suppose I could say the same about you except that you're a man. 'Dashingly attractive' would be more appropriate. And 'good evening' to you." She smiled and gave a short nod of her head.

He was wearing the latest evening dress shirt with a banded collar which he had bought in San Francisco and a thin black bowless evening tie through which ran thin lines of red, white, and green.

When he took her arm, his hand touched the sheerest, softest cashmere. He noticed the huge garnet ring as she drew the shawl from around her shoulders; on the high neck of her dress sat a thick snakelike Bulgari choker with intricately worked pearls, tiny emeralds, baguettes, rubies, and lapis set in gold.

97

It's expensive enough for Cleopatra to have had one just like it, he thought. *Beautiful. She's so beautiful. And she's still single. There must be someone outside of the college. Maybe in Maine. She's a very private person. All anyone knows is that her family is old Kennebunk. That sort of speaks wealth. And wealthy people lead quiet and private lives. Normally, they don't mix their business lives with their private lives. Are you hearing me, Sister Angela?*

Rex handed the volunteer their tickets and gave her his last name.

"Thank you, Mr. and Mrs. Borden."

Lizbeth and Rex smiled at each other.

Rex said, "Don't I wish."

Preceding him into the foyer of the main dining room, Lizbeth pretended not to hear his remark.

A waiter approached them with a silver tray of champagne flutes.

As they took a glass, Rex said, "I understand the crowd is estimated to be three-hundred-fifty."

Lizbeth lifted her glass to him and they clinked.

"For a great cause," she said.

She sipped.

"Very nice brut."

"Of course. Korbel of California," he said.

Tuxedoed waiters of both sexes, wearing white gloves, offered trays of hors d'oeuvres and small symbolic rainbow napkins.

They sipped their champagne and occasionally took an hors d'oeuvre.

"It's wonderful to think everything is unselfishly donated. Even the hotel kitchen and this banquet room. There's not one cent of overhead and all monies go toward the AIDS foundation here in Monterey."

"I guess I never heard of it because I was already back East, especially if it falls at this time in December each year. This is the latest I've stayed."

"I remember one year, I've forgotten which, they had a silent auction which featured cooking aprons signed by famous stars, including Elizabeth Taylor and k.d. lang."

People were beginning to move among the thirty round, draped and flower-centerpieced tables looking for their pre-assigned seats.

Rex looked at his ticket stubs. They were at table twelve. As they moved through the tables, they passed a center stage set up for after-dinner entertainment. At table twelve, their seats faced the front of the room from where they had just come; they could see all of the guests wending and weaving their ways to their tables.

Rex draped Lizbeth's shawl over the back of her chair. She wore no jewelry over her tight long sleeves.

Lizbeth's mouth went dry and she felt herself pale. Coming toward her, four tables away, was Gillian, escorted by a handsome man in his forties with healthily shining, curly black hair—almost as if it had been permed—and a masculinely square face with sparkling brown eyes. To worsen matters, they sat facing Lizbeth and Rex. Lizbeth could see the almost audible intake of Gillian's breath when Gillian looked up and saw her. Gillian had folded her hands in front of her, and Lizbeth glimpsed rings on her left hand. Gillian never wore jewelry except for the large amethyst on her ring finger when she wasn't wearing gloves while golfing.

Tonight, she wore at least a karat diamond and a platinum band of baguettes which shot sparkling blue-white lasers under the bright chandeliers.

* * * * *

For Christmas dinner, Gerald and Marion always went to The Covey. Walking into Quail Lodge at Christmastime was an almost reverent experience for them. The paneled lobby was festooned and the square pillars were wrapped with garlands of holly and pine; a joyously large Christmas tree trimmed elegantly in gold and red bows and ornaments greeted them. As they walked up the steps to the restaurant, they passed a great glass-lined silver wassail bowl of aromatically spicy, steaming punch with silver punch cups and white cloth napkins arranged invitingly alongside. A dark brandy-soaked fruitcake lay sliced beside it with silver forks and square silver dessert plates.

They turned left at the top of the stairs and were greeted by Thamin, the gracious, swarthily handsome maitre'd.

"Merry Christmas, Professor and Mrs. Ritchey. How wonderful to see you again."

He shook hands with Gerald, and Marion extended hers to him. Thamin held it softly between both of his.

"What a memory you have, Thamin."

"Thank you, Mrs. Ritchey. As always, it's our pleasure to host you. Professor Ritchey is a legend among our staff whose sons and daughters he has taught. I have your usual place in front of the fire."

They followed him into the lounge.

"Oh, Thamin, thank you."

They had sat only a few minutes when a soft-spoken blond attendant arrived with two perfect Manhattans—Marion's straight up and Gerald's on the rocks.

"Compliments of the house," she said.

They thanked her; they didn't talk except for their simultaneously spoken wish before they sipped: "To another Christmas together."

They sat like lovers holding hands before the fire, their drinks on the polished table before them.

When they finished their drinks, Thamin led them down the steps to the far left window to table fourteen; from there they could see the lighted fountain in the lake, the bridge over it, and occasional lights from cars piercing the night as they passed on the valley road.

Traditionally, they had a bottle of champagne with Christmas dinner; Thamin recommended number 166, the Moet & Chandon "White Star."

They had a Caesar salad concocted masterfully at tableside by Thamin and moved to their entrée—a rare rack of lamb. They talked little throughout their meal except to discuss its consistent excellence. Thamin stopped by to inquire about their meal and to refill their flutes.

When the table was cleared and brushed, and dessert declined momentarily, they discussed things both had had on their minds.

"Well," Marion said, without making a definite reference, "Mother used to say that no news is good news."

Gerald moved his flute in a nervous little circle on the cloth. Marion thought she detected a bead of sweat just below his hairline.

"Here's to Mother," he said, toasting the air and sipping.

This brought a smile to Marion's face as she slipped her hand across the table and pressed his lovingly for a moment.

"I haven't told you yet, but I dread the new semester, Marion."

"For heaven's sake, Gerald, why?"

"For one thing, evaluation."

"Gerald, you're one of the best teachers on campus. Why should you worry? You'll fly through with the students as you always do. You'll be fine," Marion assured him.

I hope so. And Jesse Keller is not exactly a supporter of mine. I don't know why, but he isn't. Something ridiculously personal. Could it be that he knows I'm a better, more efficient, and more knowledgeable teacher than he is—even if he is the chair? That's possible. He visited one of my classes as a peer evaluator when he first came here. He would never accept my request again. I can't believe that's the reason. It's so unprofessional. No, there must be something else. My ratings, when I'm visited by my colleagues, are always in the top five percent. Maybe in all of his years as a teacher, he has never been rated in that upper percentage. Some people are good administrators, some are good teachers. Often, they don't overlap. Maybe that's what he resents. God knows I could never be an administrator.

"And if your book is accepted...?"

"If," Gerald said.

She reached across to him again. "It *will* be," she said emphatically. "You can't *ever* think it won't be. I won't let you think that. You've worked too hard for too, too long. Only good can come of such honest work. It's brilliant. I say that not because you're my husband and I love you, but because I have faith in your talent. Besides, there hasn't been as good or as intelligently written a book as yours on the *Times* bestseller list in at least two years."

Gerald reached for her hand, held it, and kissed the palm.

"I love you, Marion. Always remember that."

"Are you going somewhere?" she asked.

* * * * *

When Edward awakened at six o'clock on Christmas morning, the thought of being without Sheila for almost a month kept him from going back to sleep. He got up, showered and shaved, and dressed in slacks and a mock turtleneck before he went to make coffee. He lit the fire and sat drinking coffee and staring at the packages on the floor beside the coffee table until Sarah came from her room in her robe.

When she saw him, she smiled and said, "Merry Christmas, Edward."

He arose and kissed her on the cheek after she sat in her wing chair.

"Merry Christmas, Sarah."

"A fire, Edward. How nice. You must have been up for a while."

"I have been. Since six. I couldn't sleep any longer. I'll get your juice and coffee."

"Thank you."

He returned with the juice and coffee on a tray and set the tray on the coffee table.

She sipped her juice.

Edward went to the kitchen to refill his cup and returned with the cup and a large Christmas envelope and opener which he set beneath the poinsettia on the table.

They had no tree but, to exude a Christmasy atmosphere, Edward always bought magnificent, huge poinsettias at Thursday's Monterey Peninsula College Farmer's Market and placed one on either side of the hearth, as well as one in the center of the coffee table.

Traditionally, they opened their gifts on Christmas morning after their juice and during their coffee.

She set down the empty juice glass and picked up her coffee mug. After she took a few sips and set the cup down, Edward handed her the card and opener.

She opened the envelope and withdrew the card; a letter fell into her lap.

She read the card and unfolded the letter.

Her face glowed from the festive fire and her inner joy.

"Edward, do you realize how long it's been since I've been away from here? Five days in San Francisco! The concert! The restaurants! The city at Christmas! Oh, Edward, I'll feel alive again! Come here. Let me kiss you, my love!"

He went to her and stooped; she pulled his head down to hers and, with both palms on his cheeks, kissed him long and tenderly on the lips.

Wearing a weak smile, he withdrew and returned to his seat.

"Now you," she said, and she handed him a large Neiman Marcus box from beside the coffee table—one of many which Lela had purchased at her request.

* * * * *

They stayed at the Mark Hopkins; in early November, Edward had called and requested the same room in which he and Sheila had stayed in mid-September—the difference, of course, was that he and Sheila shared one bed and he and Sarah slept in separate beds.

They taxied around the city. In Ghirardelli Square they had *Paprikasch* and hot, crusty home-made bread on the wrought iron balcony of a Hungarian restaurant on the fifth floor of a red-brick building overlooking the bay.

Walking through the shopping square, they passed a jewelry shop in which she wanted to browse. Edward was certain that the clerk would not remember him, but he stayed outside while Sarah shopped. She wanted to buy him something—either personal or for his office. She looked at crystal pieces from Orrefors, Baccarat, and Lalique which she admired; and figurines from Lladró which she thought were not masculine enough. She was smitten by a sparkling multifaceted crystal Aphrodite from Austria.

"I'll take that," she told the clerk as she handed her the Visa card. It meant love—the love they had shared and the love they had now rediscovered. It would be a talisman for their future life together which was starting right now in San Francisco.

* * * * *

The holidays in Hays, Kansas, were briefer than even *they* had anticipated. The overt awakening on the faces of Traci's parents when they met Rutland in the driveway prepared them for a short stay.

Traci kissed her mother and father and introduced Rutland to Florence and Nelson.

Grant Wood must have used them fifty years ago as models for his famous emaciated couple; the only differences were that they were much heavier because the times were more prosperous and they were more well fed. Florence had a pink bouffant hairdo, and Nelson wore

103

a bow tie, suspenders, and had a paunch. Neither offered a hand to Rutland; they just nodded with the thin veneer of a half smile on their lips. Rutland instinctively felt the rejection and didn't offer his hand either. The situation was more awkward than Traci could ever have imagined. They all just stood there, exhaling frosty plumes, until Traci said, "It's chilly. Go on in. We'll bring our bags."

Traci looked at Rutland and said, "It's chilly in more ways than one."

They took their bags from the trunk and went into the house.

"I've fixed the guest room for your friend," Florence said.

"Oh," said Traci, "thank you, Mother."

"Come on, Rutland, let's go up and freshen ourselves."

Carrying both bags, he followed Traci up the carpeted stairs.

In her room, after the door was closed, Traci said, "Shit! Has prejudice ever been more obvious?"

Her bedroom was a large bed-sitting room with a private bath. There were two upholstered chairs with a two-tiered cherrywood table between them; it was crowded with framed childhood-through-adolescence photos of Traci.

Still holding the suitcases, Rutland said, "God, I feel like I'm in a garden. There are flowers everywhere. Don't the birds keep you awake?"

Traci let out a whoop and laughed heartily, her hand hastily covering her mouth to stifle it.

"I never thought about it."

Pink flowered wallpaper, upholstery, bed cover—even the towels in the bath were pink and flowered. When Rutland pointed to the pink toilet tissue, Traci put her hand over his mouth to stifle a shriek of laughter.

Turning back into the room and noticing it for the first time, Rutland said, "And a four-poster. At least it doesn't have a frilly flowered canopy over it."

Traci said, "The guest room bed does."

Rutland rolled his eyes, and Traci kissed him.

"Come on. Grab your suitcase and I'll show you to your quarters, sir." They went out, passed a central bath, to the room opposite.

"This is the Blue Boy room," Traci said.

"I didn't know you had a brother."

This was the blue cornflower room. Whereas Traci's room had pink carpeting, Rutland's had baby blue. A print of Gainsborough's *Blue Boy* was centered on one wall. The cornflower wallpaper continued in the bathroom where it met the pale blue tile midway up the wall. On the floor was a fluffy blue rug. And in the holder near the toilet was blue toilet tissue.

Rutland pointed at the paper dispenser, disbelieving his eyes, his mouth aghast.

She laughed aloud and kissed his open mouth.

"I'll see you in a few minutes. Come over to my room if you finish before me."

They opened their luggage in their rooms and hung the few things that needed to shed wrinkles; the rest they put into drawers. The empty suitcases were stored out of sight in the bottom of their closets. They freshened themselves, leaving their rooms at the same time, kissed in the hall, and went down to the family.

It was four o'clock.

Florence was in the kitchen, putting a trussed pale yellow chicken into the oven. Nelson was twisting the metal cap on a gallon jug of Gallo red wine.

"I hope you like bur-*gun*dy red wine," Nelson said to no one in particular as the aluminum cap came off.

"We like white or red," Traci said.

Nelson poured the wine into three tumblers and said, "Ice?"

Traci and Rutland looked at each other.

Traci said, "I don't think so." *God,* she thought, *this is almost as bad as honey daiquiris!*

He handed each of them one and dropped several ice cubes into his tumbler.

"What about Mother?" Traci asked.

"Mother doesn't drink when she's cooking. She's a real gourmett."

He enunciated the word as if it were spelled with two t's.

"I'm sorry," Traci said as she looked at Rutland. Rutland knew what she meant, but Nelson thought she was sorry that Florence didn't drink while she was cooking.

My God! Traci thought, *haven't they heard of Julia Child and 'Cook's Nips'? Everything is better when the cook has had a few.*

105

Look at the way Julia says: 'Add about a half cup of wine' and while she's talking, more than half a bottle glugs into whatever she's making. And then, with parched lips as she takes another sip from a good Sonoma, she says: 'It's delicious.' What? The wine or the beef? Haven't Julia's tapes been seen in Kansas? Oh, Dorothy, did you take everything away to Oz?

"We're having chicken, mashed potatoes, and creamed peas," Florence said. "Oh, yes, there's also a salad. Lemon Jell-O with grated carrots on chopped iceberg. It's so colorful. Almost Christmasy. I'm sure this will be a change from grits and greens."

Traci and Rutland looked at each other.

Rutland said, "Oh, thank you. You know, I've never tried grits or greens. Where I was raised, they were legendary; no one ever ate them."

Florence and Nelson smiled at each other, pleased that they had chosen the perfect menu for their first evening meal.

"We'll be eating by five-fifteen. I hope that's not too late?"

"Not at all," said Rutland.

What the fuck do we do the rest of the evening? Traci thought.

As if Florence read her thought, she said "There's *Wheel of Fortune* and some wonderful reruns of Archie Bunker which we always watch, isn't there, Nelson?"

"Oh, yes, Mother."

Oh, Christ! thought Traci.

Haven't heard 'Mother' since 'Daddy' called her that in Albee's The Sandbox, thought Rutland as he smiled at Traci.

Then, to Nelson, she said, "I'd like a tumblerful more of that bur-*gun*dy red wine. Make it full, please. And no ice."

Dinner was eaten.

"It doesn't look like Christmas, does it, Traci? I mean, we don't have a tree or nothing. Not even *one* poinset-tia. Did I say that right? Some people call it a poinset-ta. Why would they have a 'i' in it and not pernounce it right? But Dad and I got rid of all the ornaments and everything else at a yard sale this past summer. We figured we'd never do a tree again. It's too much work to put up and take down. I mean, the lights and all."

Dessert was tapioca pudding with mushy defrosted raspberries.

Florence swallowed a spoonful and, looking at Traci, said, "How do you like your new apartment?"

"We love it, don't we, Rutland?"

Silence prevailed.

The ceiling fell.

Oh, shit, I did it!

As Rutland and Traci looked at each other across the table, they were aware of Florence and Nelson doing the same

"Would you like coffee? I'll make some if you want. Dad and I don't drink coffee at night because it keeps us awake."

"Us, too," Traci said.

There was silence again.

The roof fell through the ceiling.

"Well, then," Florence said, clearing her throat noisily and placing her napkin on the table, "I'll clean up the table and Dad will help me with the dishes."

"No, no. I think Dad and Rutland should go into the living room and relax and that you and I should get the kitchen in order. That way they can get to know each other better."

Florence cleared her throat again. "Yes, well, then...."

"Let's go," Traci finished for her.

* * * * *

Christmas was two days away. When Florence and Nelson went to bed, Traci—remembering the two-hour time difference and using her MCI card—called Gerald and Marion to wish them a Merry Christmas and to ask a favor of them: Call the day after Christmas and say that it's urgent that they return. She, Traci, would invent some reason, but what she needed was a phone call. Marion asked no questions. They would do as they were asked. Meanwhile, Traci also called the airlines and—fortunately—was able to change their flight. This was between the holidays, said the agent, and seats were available.

* * * * *

Gillian heard the garage door slide open as she sat in the den having a vodka martini on the rocks and watching Peter Jennings on the 5:30 news.

Ralph came into the kitchen from the garage and called to her: "Hello. I'm home."

Gillian appeared in the kitchen, drink in hand. "You're a little late tonight."

"I was working with a new contractor who'll be giving us lots of business."

"Good."

Gillian went to the freezer and took out a pitcher of martinis and an ice-filled glass and poured his drink. She speared two garlic-stuffed olives from the open bottle on the counter and dropped them into it. He never ate them. She filled her glass and added another lemon twist.

They clinked their glasses and sipped; following her into the den and holding the drink in his left hand, he loosened his tie and unbuttoned his collar with the other. She had turned down the sound by remote when she went to greet Ralph and now Peter was solemnly, soundlessly giving the Dow-Jones Industrial Average and the NASDAQ Index for the day. Both, they read in the captions, were down.

They sat, turned on the sound, and continued to watch.

When Peter signed off, Ralph unknotted his tie and let it hang.

"Golf today?"

"Yes."

"Good?"

"Under par."

"Again?"

She didn't respond.

"Something wrong?"

She wiggled her glass so that the ice cubes clinked against it.

"My regular golf partner hasn't been there."

"Oh? Can't you play with someone else? I mean, I don't know anything about golf."

"I do, but it's not the same." Looking into the bottom of her glass as she barely sipped her drink, she added, "We need to talk, Ralph."

He turned and looked at her.

"This sounds serious."

"It is."

"Could I shower and change first?"

"Of course. That would be better anyway. It would give me time to organize my confused thoughts."

He rose and stood looking down at her.

Her legs curled on the sofa, her right arm on the back of it, she was staring into her glass.

He finished the martini and held his glass out to her. "Would you pour me another drink?"

She leaned over to set her glass on the coffee table and took his. When he left, she uncurled herself and went into the kitchen. She took the icy pitcher from the freezer, poured the remainder into Ralph's glass, and added cubes from the ice bucket on the butcher block counter. From the cupboard beside the refrigerator, she took a bottle of Skyy; without measuring, she poured the vodka into the pitcher. From the refrigerator, she took a bottle of dry vermouth and waved it unopened over the mouth of the pitcher.

She smiled to herself at that idiotic action before she put the pitcher in the freezer and the vermouth in the refrigerator.

Beginning to smell her casserole baking, she crossed the kitchen, opened the oven door, took the potholder that was lying on the counter, slid the rack out far enough for her to remove the lid, and stirred the bubbling casserole with a wooden spoon; she set the lid on the rack beside the casserole and tested the meat with a long-handled fork. At least another hour before it was finished. She laid the fork and spoon in the spoonholder, put on the lid, slid the rack into place, and closed the oven door.

Just enough time to tell Ralph what she wanted him to know.

She walked back to get Ralph's drink and was suddenly aware that she was still carrying the potholder. She had a brief stab of anxiety under her heart and felt herself flush. She placed her hands flat on the counter and leaned her forehead against the cabinet for a few seconds to regain control. When she felt steady enough, she picked up Ralph's drink, laid the potholder on the other counter beside the fork and spoon, and walked into the den.

Ralph had finished showering; she heard the soft whoosh of the sliding mirrored doors in the bedroom. Perched on the sofa, she took a

109

hearty sip of her martini as Ralph entered in chinos and a blue but-
ton-down collar shirt; his black, curly hair was still damp and she
could smell his Givenchy cologne.

"Thanks," he said as he sat in the upholstered chair at the side of
the coffee table so he could face her as they talked.

"Ralph, there's something which has been bothering me for the
past months."

"I know. I've felt it."

"Please, Ralph, let me talk. I'm having a hard enough time
bringing myself to this."

"Okay."

Words tumbled out, not necessarily coherently. "About six
months ago, when I switched from Rancho Cañada to The Ranch, I
met someone while I was playing golf. We've seen each other and
played golf together as often as possible during the past months. You
couldn't have known because I made sure I was home in plenty of
time before you got home."

Ralph sat up straighter in the chair, preparing to ward off
something he wasn't ready for. He took a sip of his drink and
swallowed noisily; it was as if he were ingesting a whole olive instead
of liquid.

"I never thought it could happen to me. It was so sudden. I was in
torment for a while. I couldn't let myself think it was real. Nothing
physical happened for a month. I was the one who instigated it. I
couldn't help myself."

Gillian couldn't stop the rapid fire choppy sentences which rushed
from her. She had to get the words out fast or she wouldn't be able to
get through this, and she wanted to be honest.

Ralph stood up. "You what? Did I hear what I think I did? You
slept with someone else?"

She looked up at him and started to cry.

"Ralph. Ralph, I don't want to hurt you."

"That's a helluva thing to say! What do you think you're doing
anyway? Giving me a belated Christmas gift or a good start for the
new year?"

"I'm sorry."

"Is that all you have to say? You're sorry? For what you did?
You're sorry?"

Then, in a low monotone, he continued. "You should be. I don't want to hear 'I'm sorry' one more time. 'Sorry' isn't enough! You're not sorry you enjoyed it though, are you?"

"Oh, Ralph, I nearly went crazy over this. I didn't know what to do."

Her voice cracked.

"You managed to work it out for yourself, though, didn't you? And to your advantage?"

"No, Ralph, you've got to believe me. I wrestled with my mind. I tried to tell myself it was wrong. I never thought I'd be in this situation. We've had eight wonderful years of marriage."

Tears streamed down her cheeks; she wiped them with the back of her hand.

Ralph picked up his drink and drained it before he announced that he needed another one and took long strides toward the kitchen.

Gillian went into the powder room and got some tissues. She was on the sofa again when he returned.

"Is he from Monterey?"

Gillian looked up into his eyes but didn't answer immediately.

"Well, is he?"

"No." After what seemed an hour's pause, she wrenched the words from her throat: "It's a woman."

Ralph was stunned. His eyes never left hers. His mouth dropped open. With dreamlike, slow, measured movements, he sat down in his chair, legs apart, his hands drooping between them; after an eternity of silence, he placed his glass on the table.

"Oh, Ralph, it isn't that I don't love you. I do. Please try to understand."

He stared at her without seeing her cry or wipe her eyes. Then, flatly, he said: "I married a lesbian."

"No!" Gillian cried.

Ralph's voice was a monotone when he said, "What are you then, if not that? You slept with a woman."

"Yes, but I've never slept with a woman before. Believe me. This just happened. Believe me."

"Nothing ever *just happens,* Gillian." He finally blinked his eyes. "Oh, I see, you're telling me that in order to be a lesbian, you have to keep a scorecard. Is that it?"

111

"I've never touched another girl in my life. I've never slept with another girl even innocently at pajama parties. I can't explain why I'm drawn to her."

He turned away, unable to look at her.

"A lesbian. *Me* for another woman. I don't understand this at all. No matter what you say to me. It's unnatural. A woman having sex with another woman. What do you do?"

Gillian covered her face with her hands and wept, her body shaking. When she was able to control herself, she looked up at him, almost beseechingly.

"She didn't instigate it, Ralph. She's a beautiful woman. I didn't want to let go."

"*You* didn't want to let go?" He turned to look down at her when another thought hit him. "How old *is* she?"

"Thirty one."

"And does she have a husband who's facing the same ugliness I am?"

"She's not married. And it's not ugly."

"A true dyke, then."

"How dare you use such a denigrating word! You don't even know her."

"I know enough! She's stolen my wife!"

"Ralph, I don't want to hurt you. I *am* sorry and I still love you in a very special way. How could I *not* love you?"

"You tell *me*! Sounds like a song out of the eighties about someone having two lovers. How can you love two people of two different sexes at the same time?"

"I don't know, but I do."

"Who *is* this mystery woman?"

"She's a professor at the college."

"Are you equivalent to her mentally? Don't forget, you only went to high school." His voice affected a low, mocking sneer, when he said, "Or is it the physical aspect that's more important? What do you do anyway?"

"Oh, Ralph, don't make this something ugly."

"Ha! It's heaven for you. What is it for me?"

He had forgotten his drink. Now he remembered it and downed it in one draught.

"What's her name?"

"Why?"

"Why? Some woman professor has stolen my wife from me and I can't ask who she is?"

"I'm afraid you'll do something to her."

"And why shouldn't I? Look what she's done to me!"

"Ralph, if I tell you, please don't do anything to her. Hurt me in some way, but not her. Please? If you love me as you say you do, then you'll listen to reason."

"Reason? Listen to who's talking about reason?"

He waved his empty glass above her bowed head.

"I need another drink. How about you? Maybe I can get you drunk and convince you that I'm better than her."

Gillian turned her head away and wept into her arm.

She forgave him, though, because she understood the shock and pain he was experiencing.

When he returned with an iceless tumblerful, he began again.

"You still haven't told me her name."

"Why must you know?"

"I think I'm entitled to know. Wouldn't you feel you were entitled to know if I left you for another woman...or man?" He threw back his head. "Oh, my God!"

Anxiety.

She didn't want to tell him.

He pressed her for an answer.

"Lizbeth Rostrand."

"Quite an elegant name."

"She is."

"I see. And you're not out of your element?"

"She doesn't think so."

"How do you feel about this?"

"As breathtakingly beautiful as she is."

"Thanks. That's some mix."

"Ralph, you're making this into something uglier than I ever dreamed it could be."

"*I* am?"

"Yes."

"I'm sorry then for both of us. If we're hurt, that's all that matters. You're a lesbian in the eyes of the world. And you've left me for another woman. I'm filing for divorce, and don't you even try to get one penny from me."

"I don't want anything from you, Ralph. You gave me beautiful years."

"So you say!"

He took a hearty sip of his drink.

"Then why this?"

She looked up at him through tears.

"I'm sorry I've hurt you, Ralph. I don't want anything from you. I have good memories of our life together. I have no regrets."

"Wait a minute. Regrets? About me or her?"

"About us."

"Which *us* ? Me and you, or you and her?"

"However I answer will be wrong."

"You bet. One other thing. When I was on trips, did you spend the nights together?"

"Yes."

"Where?" Then, as a horrid possibility suddenly hit him, he shrieked, "Here?"

"No, at her place."

"Thank God! If she had, I'd have burned the mattress!"

Gillian looked at him with tear-reddened eyes; to take her gaze from his, she set her glass on the table and looked down at her folded hands.

"Did she know about me?"

As she shook her head, she said, "Not until the AIDS benefit."

Ralph stared at her. "What do you mean? 'Until the AIDS benefit?'" He mimicked her in an angry, insulting falsetto.

"She saw me there with you."

"Have you seen her since."

"No."

"Why not?"

"She's gone back to visit her parents for the holidays."

"Then you've been living lies all these months! And you still are!"

Gillian said nothing, but she nodded her bowed head.

"How can you look in the mirror at your deceitful face?"

114

He finished the martini and set the glass down on the table with a glass-on-glass thud.

"Oh, my God! What a twisted life you've been living! I should feel sorry for you, instead of hating you."

He stood before her; from beneath her lowered eyes, she could see his hands fisted at his sides.

"Don't you want dinner?"

"I don't want anything touched by you. And from now on, I sleep in the guest room. And I want you out of my house and my sight as soon as possible. No! Sooner! Go live with your dyke friend! See how long it lasts! But get this straight. I'm not done with you and your dyke friend. You'll be sorry you ever met each other before I'm finished. You don't fuck me like this and get away with it. Either of you!"

He moved closer, now towering over her quailing head.

"Happy New Year, lesbian!"

He spat on the floor, turned and walked into the kitchen for another drink.

PART II

Some Questions, Some Answers

January, 1999

Chapter 7

THE COLLEGE WAS CLOSED from December 15th until January 12th, but administrators and faculty could work in their offices beginning the Monday after the new year. The mailroom crew also worked because of the pile-up of first class, junk mail, and complimentary copies of new texts which had to be delivered several times a day until the mailroom was cleared.

It arrived among the books and mail. Gerald tried to ignore its presence by looking at the junk mail and discarding it quickly; by opening the first class mail—reading it, stapling the envelope to the letter, and placing it in his "in" box; by tearing open the brown boxes and padded bags of complimentary copies of new texts he looked at in the fall; then by bravely attacking the box whose contents he knew. *They didn't even FedEx it.* He paused. *What's wrong with me? The college was closed.*

He looked at the postal date. It was sent December 16th, so it had lain in the main post office waiting for the college mail room to open.

Just as well, he thought, *it would have ruined Christmas. At least not knowing—as Marion had said—gave him a sense of hope. So. Let's see how this year will begin.*

A letter was enclosed.

Dear Professor Ritchey:

Thank you for sending your manuscript to Bill Slater and for giving us an early opportunity to read it.

You have written quite a tome which held my interest and the interest of several colleagues; however, its length is somewhat intimidating for most readers of fiction.

Your range of characters is wonderfully drawn, and your plot is intricate enough to have the reader turn pages to just beyond midway. Then it slows down and the reader is no longer as intrigued to know the outcome; there are just too many more pages. Even one of our readers began to skip to the end.

As an editor, I know how much work and time have gone into this effort. But, as an editor, I also know that the general reading public cannot handle the length.

Therefore, I would like to make a suggestion. Could you— somehow—perhaps create two volumes out of this? The work on the second half as a sequel would require quite a bit of rewriting and the end of the first volume would have to be reworked.

We're sorry that we are unable to work with the manuscript as submitted. Let us hear from you.

Sincerely,

Rita Lore

Rita Lore
Editor-in-Chief
Fiction Department

Disappointing, yet encouraging, he thought. *But, no, I won't create two volumes, and I cannot take the time to rewrite an ending and to lengthily revise the second volume. Someone somewhere will see its worth and take it as it is.*

He called Marion. When she answered, he said, "Well, it's back."

"And?"

"The letter's negative in one way and encouraging in another."

He read it to her.

When he finished, she said, "What are you going to do?"

"Be stubborn," he said. "I'll wait for one of the other reps to come around in February or March."

"Darling, as long as you believe in yourself and your work, success *will* come. *I* believe that and I know *you* do."

"Thank you, Marion. Don't forget. I need your strength, too."

"That you always have, and you know it."

"Marion, we won't say anything to anyone just yet."

"Now, Gerald. Who needs to know what? Of course not. Just finish up what you have to do and come home. We'll have a nice glass of wine and I'll hold your hand. Does that tempt you?"

"Oh, Marion. I love you."

She blew a kiss into the phone.

He puckered his lips, but no sound came.

When they hung up, he held his head in his hands; he tried to stifle the tears.

* * * * *

The phone rang. Edward answered. The voice on the other end scorched the pit of his stomach.

"When did you get back?"

He looked at his desk calendar; it was the tenth of January. He looked at his watch; it was close to noon.

"About twenty minutes ago. I'm at my parents' place in Monterey picking up my car. Then I'm heading home."

She was silent a minute before she said, "Did you miss me?"

All he could answer was a drawn out "Oh" as a sigh.

She blew a kiss into the phone. "I've come back to you."

"How was your trip?"

121

"I have an all-over tan."

After a moment, he said, "What are you telling me?"

"Don't you want to see it before it fades?"

"You know I do. Can't wait."

"Tonight?"

"This afternoon?"

"Short notice. I have to unpack and get things ready. Classes start in two days."

"How about tomorrow? Lunch? And after?"

"Sounds great."

"Don't wash off all the tan before I see it," he said.

"Where should I meet you?"

"Park on the side of The Running Iron and I'll pick you up there at eleven-thirty."

"Can't wait. Love you."

She hung up.

He sat with his mouth open, in shock rather than in response. He was thoughtless for a moment. *This had taken an all-new direction. There wasn't supposed to be love involved. I thought it was only sex. Now that I think of it, I guess I'm feeling more than I ever could. I did miss her. It wasn't until she called that I realized how much.*

* * * * *

Gillian slowed and stopped at the gate in her silver 560 SL Mercedes. She saw Lizbeth's silver Jaguar parked in the courtyard near the bubbling fountain. She pressed the button on the phone; it rang and then Lizbeth's soft voice asked: "Who is it?"

"It's me," she said.

"Who is 'me'?"

"Lizbeth, it's Gillian."

There was no answer; it seemed an eternity before the buzzer sounded and the gate swung open.

Gillian's wheels spun on the gravel as she pulled through the gate and parked alongside the Jaguar.

The front door did not swing open before her arrival as it always had.

Gillian rang the bell. Even then, it was a tantalizing space of time before the great carved mahogany door swung inward.

Lizbeth stood poised and chic in black spandex slacks and a black silk short-sleeved polo blouse. She was sheer elegance as usual. Her champagne hair was fluffed as if she had just brushed it. If *Architectural Digest* ever used models in their spectacular settings, she looked as if she belonged in one.

"How are you? I haven't seen you for a while."

"I'm fine. That's why I'm here," Gillian explained. "May I come in?"

"Certainly. Any time."

Gillian walked past Lizbeth. There was only the empty sound of the gurgling fountain in the entrance hall; there was no longer laughter in its spill.

She stood there.

"You know where the living room is—or have you forgotten?"

Gillian didn't answer.

She walked between Richard MacDonald's two life-size bronzes of *Diana, Huntress*—on low pedestals of cream-veined brown Carrara—through the open doors to the living room and stood, like a stranger, just inside.

Lizbeth followed and then preceded her to the pair of sofas flanking the fireplace. She motioned for Gillian to sit on the other sofa; between them on the carved mahogany coffee table lounged Loet Vanderveen's family of magnificent cheetahs.

"How were your holidays?"

"Pensive," Lizbeth said.

Guilt made Gillian's head bow. She looked at her fingers; in the absence of the amethyst, a white space circled her finger.

"Haven't you forgotten something?" Lizbeth asked.

"Please don't do this to me," Gillian said.

"Why did you come here? It's nearly five weeks since I saw you at The Doubletree."

Lizbeth's voice was less than cordial; the warm, soft timbre was missing and Gillian was uncomfortable in its absence.

Defensively, Gillian said, "You've been away."

"But, before that. I've been miserable not seeing you, Gillian. And I've been home since January second. It's now the tenth."

123

"How could I know?" Looking into Lizbeth's eyes, she said, "Can we stop this?"

"I was hoping you would call me the morning after the benefit. After your husband had gone to work."

"Lizbeth, I was a mess. All I could do was cry. I was angry with myself for not having told you that I was married. But I couldn't be sure of anything. Not even myself. Was this maybe just a fling which would go away? I've never been in love with a woman before. All of this was new to me. How did I know you wouldn't get tired of me? Then what would I have? I'd be hurt. I'd have hurt Ralph. Everything could have been a worse mess."

"Didn't it ever occur to you that I was hurt?"

Tears welled in Gillian's eyes.

"I was attracted to you like I've never been attracted to anyone but Ralph. When I met you, everything changed."

Gillian stood up and went to her. She lifted Lizbeth's slender hands from her knees and took them in hers.

"Lizbeth, I needed time to think. I've been so confused. I told Ralph just before the new year. I had to. It wasn't a pretty scene. He's noticed the difference in me and my behavior with him for months. I don't want to hurt him any more than I have. He's a fine man and I still love him, but I know now that I love you more."

Lizbeth sat back against the cushions. Gillian sat on the edge of the sofa, facing her. Their eyes were searching each other's as they spoke.

"I can understand that, Gillian. Why didn't you ever talk to me about this? Why didn't you ever tell me you were married? Why did you lie to me? Oh, so many lies. I'd have bowed out of your life before our relationship was too far along."

"That's why I didn't. That's why I lied. Believe me, it was hard living a lie, but I didn't want to lose you."

"I've lived here five years now. The first winter I returned home for Christmas, I heard about the lesbian world in Santa Cruz when I was at a bar in Kennebunk. I bought a gay guide in Boston and, when I returned to the Valley, I drove up the coast one Friday night and met someone. She was a French professor at the university there. We had a two-year relationship—a lovely affair, and I thought it would work. From Friday evening until Sunday afternoon, I spent my weekends with her. The third winter while I went home to Kennebunk, she had an affair with a graduate student. When I returned, she was honest and told me about it immediately. I'm happy about that. So many people—heterosexual and homosexual—lie to each other. But she didn't. I loved her for that.

"Other than her, I've not had a relationship with anyone, male or female, until I met you. I never found anyone who appealed to me and I avoided any kind of liaison. I've gone out with men on occasion—and only one from the college—and I never permitted it to go beyond a date or two. I've never been with a woman here. This is a small community and my position at the college could be at stake."

They sat silent for a while, then Gillian moved toward Lizbeth and kissed her softly on the lips.

"Lizbeth, times have changed."

"I can't deny that I've met some wonderful lesbian couples who have been together for years and both of whom are feminine. I like that. I have friends in advertising in New York who have told me about some of the beautiful female models whom no one suspects to be lesbian and who are picked up, after the shoot, by extremely masculine women. You see, I prefer a woman to one masquerading as a man.

"It's like some of the wonderful men I know who like or love *men,* not effeminate men or men masquerading as women."

"To get back to what you said about the valley and the college," Gillian said, "no one cares about someone else's personal preference."

"Except someone's husband. What about Ralph?"

Gillian didn't answer.

"He's a very handsome man."

"Yes, he is."

"You're sure that you've come to a conclusion about yourself?"

"I have."

"What about Ralph?"

"Ralph is divorcing me."

Lizbeth took Gillian's hands and squeezed them.

"But you're still living there."

"Like strangers. He wants me to leave as soon as possible."

Lizbeth pressed them hard again, almost insistently. "Would you want to come and live with me?"

Gillian burst into tears and embraced Lizbeth who held her close and kissed her hair.

"Yes," Gillian sobbed. "Oh, yes."

They drew apart but still held each other. Lizbeth kissed Gillian's closed, wet eyelids and then her mouth.

Softly.

"What do you want to do?"

"Make love to you. I've missed you."

* * * * *

Edward turned up Via Contenta from the Valley Road and then did a quick left into the side lot of The Running Iron. He was on time, but the black Spyder was already near the side entrance. He parked beside it. She opened the door, exposed tan inner thighs, and got into the passenger side of Edward's car. She sat looking at him for a minute, placed her hand on his thigh, then slid it between his legs.

"Do we have to have lunch?"

"We'll have more energy," he said.

"If I have any more, you'll have to chain me down."

"Then, let's hurry."

They drove thirty minutes to Fisherman's Wharf in Monterey, where he parked and they descended into The Sand Dab, an intimate restaurant where they could watch the otters swimming on their backs among the parked boats and over the darting fleets of luminescent silver anchovies.

As they descended the wooden stairs, he thought he heard his name. He turned and looked, but saw no one.

They had spicy Bloody Marys, shared an appetizer of huge fried oysters, and had the namesake specialty—sautéed sand dabs—as entrées.

Afterwards, they drove back to the side entrance of The Running Iron where she picked up her car and they went to her place.

Neither could wait.

In the bedroom, they tore off each other's clothes; since she wore less, she was naked first. He scaled her body with his mouth; she moaned ecstatically. When, finally, she had him naked, she went down the length of him and enveloped him with her mouth. He threw back his head and stood solidly statuesque as she devoured him.

This was a hungry first.

When she finally released him, she said, "God, how I've missed you and your beautiful masculine body."

* * * * *

The phone rang.

"Hello, Sarah. Marion. How have you been?"

"Fine. Did you have good holidays?"

"Yes. And you?

"We went up to the city for a long weekend. The ballet, the opera, a concert, shopping. It was great. It's been a long time."

"I'm happy for you," she said.

"And what did you do?"

"Our usual. The Covey. Champagne. Gerald. What more could I ask for?"

"Why don't you come by some afternoon?"

"That was one reason I called. To see if I could and when?"

"I'd love you to. As I told you before, it gets a bit lonely for me here once in a while. When is it good for you?"

"You name it."

"Tomorrow?"

"Fine."

"About two? Lela leaves at one. We'll be alone and we can talk."

"Good. Gerald has late classes tomorrow. I'll see you then."

"Bye for now," Sarah said.

* * * * *

Even before the mail clerk handed him his packet of mail and he thanked her, Rutland saw the two large letter-size brown interoffice envelopes. He looked at the 'To...From' lines: One was from Jesse Keller, the Chair of Composition, and the other was from Mary Anne Starblack, the Chair of Literature. He lifted the Scotch-taped flap and withdrew the multicolored sheets with a brief cover memo dated two days ago.

127

To: All Composition Faculty

From: Jesse Keller, Chair of Composition $\mathcal{JK}$

Date: January 30, 1999

Subject: Spring Evaluation

Enclosed are your evaluation materials for this spring.
Please read them carefully, as they are the new procedures
established by the board.

All materials, class visits by your selected peers, and their
written evaluations of your performance must be returned
to my office before spring break, March 13th.

Please inform your peers of the deadline.

Thank you.

He sat back in his chair and perused the six forms. When he
finished, he rose, took them with him and, leaving his office door
open, went to visit Gerald.

Gerald was looking at the same sheets when Rutland entered the
office.

"What do you think?" Rutland asked.

"A lot of work to do in a month. But, what has to be done has to
be done, I guess. It's all part of the job."

"I have the same memo from Starblack."

Gerald laid his sheets on the desk.

Rutland sat in front of him.

"Tell me, how has your Wideman biography been doing?"

"Great at Berkeley and Stanford, but the East Coast sales are
incredible. At Howard University in Washington, DC, it's required
reading in every lit course. At the University of Maryland, some
professors are using it as a supplement for their American literature
course readings. NYU, Boston U., and all Ivy League schools are
adding it to their suggested reading lists. Naturally, not much in the
south, southwest, or midwest except at The University of Illinois."

"Congratulations, Rutland, I'm extremely happy for you."

"Thanks, Gerald."

He didn't ask about Gerald's work.

"Before we know it, spring break will be here. How're your classes going?"

"Never have any problems. Oh, yes, the fun of the critical biography is that my classes have bought the book for me to sign. They think I'm a celebrity."

"You are. You're the only one here published last year."

Then he said it. "And you will be this year."

"God willing."

* * * * *

Cheryl brought in the stack of late morning mail to Rex.

"Evaluation time," she said.

"I know. Not a favorite time for anyone. Even me."

"You've got nothing to worry about."

"Cheryl, you know as well as I do that there's always one unhappy Trojan out there who hates you."

"Unfairly."

"However. But that *one* is still there."

"Unfortunately. But I always say that those who know me know better. That is, the truth overcomes the viciousness and the lies."

"Administrators always hope so." Cheryl smiled, gave him a thumbs-up signal, and walked away. At the door she turned and said, "Nothing to wrinkle your brow over. The people who count know who you are."

Rex opened the brown interoffice envelope. In it was the notification that the evaluation materials enclosed had been sent to his English and Humanities faculties.

What do I have to worry about? This is ridiculous. I've always been a good administrator. I've been everything that Sister Angela beat into me. When my faculty or chairs haven't submitted materials on time, haven't I been patient, understanding, and tolerant?

There are some unhappy people out there who are very intolerant. Those who can't accept Rutland and Traci. And even Jesse Keller whose dislike of Gerald is incomprehensible and so pronounced that

129

most of the English Department recognize it and talk about it. And, ironically, the English Department considers itself to be the most liberal and understanding of all departments in the college.

Whatever happens, I must defend and protect them—individually or as a unit.

* * * * *

Michael Larson finished restocking his salad bar in the kitchen after the last lunch had been served. Bill Steck, who had trained him, arrived and put on his clean apron to take over the dinner shift. They greeted each other and Michael tossed his apron into the huge steel-rimmed drum provided for employees' soiled uniforms.

He left the restaurant by the kitchen door and went to his car. His books were on the passenger side.

Leaving the restaurant parking lot in Monterey and going south on Route 1, he thought about Sheila and the wild sex they had had until the last couple of months. Not knowing why she had shut him off so abruptly was driving him crazy.

* * * * *

Lizbeth was sitting sidewise at her desk, working at her computer, reading and correcting what was on the screen, when she felt a presence behind her at the open door of her office. She swung around and recognized the handsome dark-haired man standing there.

"So you're Professor Rostrand."

"Yes. And you're Ralph Warner, Gillian's husband."

"How do you know that?"

"I saw you at the AIDS benefit in December. That was when I learned that Gillian was married."

He grunted acknowledgment. "I'd like to come in."

"Please do."

She motioned to the armchair in front of her desk.

He sat facing her.

Lizbeth was wearing a beige and brown herringbone jacket with a long-sleeve blouse of silk Charmeuse. The deeply etched collar swept halfway to her shoulders and deep into her tanned cleavage.

After an uncomfortably long stare, he said, on an exasperated sigh, "I hate to say it, but you're as beautiful as Gillian said you were."

Lizbeth blushed almost to the color of her ivory-pink lipcream. She sat looking at her hands folded in front of her on the desk. Her slender fingers ended in nails painted the soft rose of the underlip of a conch shell. Silk cuffs protruded chicly an inch below the jacket sleeves.

"You could have any man you want. Why my wife? Why did you have to take my wife from me?"

"I didn't know about you. I was upset with her for not telling me she was married. I never would have wanted to hurt you or to have her hurt you."

Ralph looked directly into Lizbeth's eyes.

"Then why did you?"

"That's unfair. It wasn't planned. It just happened. Neither she nor I would have purposely hurt you. Gillian told you the truth."

"I can see now why it might have happened. Seeing you as you are. I just don't understand the whole thing. It's not natural."

"Neither can we understand. However, it's natural for us. We have no control over our feelings, nor do we make a choice."

"I don't believe that," Ralph said.

A tone of anger and defiance crept into his voice. "Then why did she marry me? She said she loved me at the time. How can that change? After years of what I'd like to believe was a happy married life, how can she turn into a lesbian? Tell me."

He said the word *lesbian* with bitterness. After a studied hesitation, he continued in a low, rasping voice. "I'll tell *you*. *You* changed *her*!"

Lizbeth did not want a contest. She felt pain for Ralph and imagined that she knew what frustration and helplessness he was experiencing.

His hands on the arms of the chair, he pushed himself up; he was visibly shaken and his voice betrayed his irrationality as he pointed his finger at her.

"And you teach? What? Lesbianism? You should be banned from contact with young people! You're a pervert!"

131

Lizbeth rose from her chair. In a quiet, unruffled and dignified tone, she said, "I think you had better leave."

"You bet I will. When I'm finished with you and not one minute before!"

"I don't know what there is to talk further about."

She sat.

"When she came to you this month and told you about my reaction, why didn't you break it off then?"

"Why should I? You told her to leave."

Absentmindedly, she rearranged papers on her desk.

"And you were waiting in your web for her, weren't you?"

"I won't say I was sorry to hear about her eviction and your divorce action."

"Of course not. You benefited from my reactions and decisions. They're probably what you wanted all the time—from the very beginning."

Lizbeth stared directly at him. "I don't deny that I wanted her to live with me, but that was an impossibility because of what she had led me to believe."

Ralph sat.

"Just what kinds of lies did she tell you? Whatever they were, you must be gullible or blinded by your perverted affection."

"I don't think that there is any need to discuss what we shared during the early days of our relationship."

"I guess I have to give her some credit for pulling it off on a smart professor like you." He spat out the word *professor* disdainfully.

"I don't think that was Gillian's intention."

"How would you know what her intention was? She fooled *you* for months. She fooled *both* of us for months. How can you trust her—even now?"

Ralph inched to the edge of his chair and pointed his finger at her. "Have you thought about the risk? She left me for you. It will only be a matter of time before she leaves you for another dyke."

Lizbeth inhaled deeply. On her exhale, she stood and said, "Your crudeness is tiring. I think we've said all we need to. Leave now or I'll call security."

He noticed that she was wearing a softly feminine version of men's trousers. His eyes went from her face to her trousers.

Scathingly, eyeing her casual outfit, he said, "Gladly. I can't stand being in the same room with a woman in men's clothing. A real dyke."

* * * * *

When his phone buzzed, Rex was working at his desk on the line items for the new budget which he had to present to the board before the first of June. He pressed the speaker button and Cheryl told him that a Mister Ralph Warner would like to see him.

Rex told her to send him in in a few minutes.

Well, whatever it was would take only a few minutes.

He sometimes welcomed these brief interruptions during the tedious days of budget preparation.

Besides, all of his departments had not yet presented their proposals and requests to him, so this unscheduled interruption would not pose a problem.

When the door opened, he set down the ruler he was using as a guide. He looked up and saw a serious-looking dark-haired man in his forties.

"Come in."

Rex stood and extended his hand.

The man entered and shut the door, but did not take his hand.

They looked at each other. Their shrugging shoulders provided the body language they both understood.

Cordially, Rex asked, "What can I do for you, Mr. Warner?"

He motioned for Ralph to sit.

"I prefer to stand."

"Your choice."

Rex sat.

"I have a problem with one of your professors."

"Are you the father of one of our students?"

"No. One of your professors is having an affair with my wife."

"I see," Rex said, as he tilted back in his desk chair, his hands gripping the side arms.

"Isn't that more of a personal issue between you and the professor? I'm afraid that that is not in my jurisdiction."

"I think it should be."

"Have you talked with the professor?"

"Yes."

"And?"

"She doesn't have anything to say."

"The professor? She?"

Rex leaned forward, his hands clasped in front of him on the desk.

"Professor Rostrand."

Rex displayed no reaction to Ralph's comment. He sat poised in his chair.

Thank you as always, Sister Angela, for what you taught me about understanding and tolerance.

"I know Professor Rostrand very well. I hired her when the college opened five years ago. She's a fine woman and an excellent teacher. Her students love and admire her."

"She's a lesbian."

"Mr. Warner, what has anyone's sexual preference to do with talent, education, or profession?"

Ralph stared at him without answering, then said, "You mean to tell me that you condone this sort of behavior?"

"Behavior? What do you mean 'behavior'? What I believe is that all of us have our lives to live according to what has been determined to make us happy and complete. Who should judge anyone? I won't. Should you?"

"I can see that talking with you is getting me nowhere?"

Rex looked at him and shook his head. He leaned farther forward across his desk and said, "Where do you want to go?"

Ralph stood.

"To the president of the college."

"His office is three doors down."

Rex stood, came around the desk, and went toward the door.

Ralph was there first and opened it.

"Be my guest, Mr. Warner."

In the outer office, Cheryl swung around when she heard Rex. Upon seeing the two men, she returned to her work.

Without a word, Ralph slammed the door behind him.

* * * * *

134

Lizbeth picked up the phone. It was Cheryl, Rex's secretary, who told her that he would like her to come to his office if she was free.

She was still shaken from her encounter with Ralph; she stood for a second to gather her composure, took her keys from her desk top, walked slowly to her office door, closed and locked it.

Every movement was measured.

Rex's office was two buildings away with the other administrators' offices. Hastening up the sidewalk, she was greeted by students. She smiled and returned their greetings, but her mind was on other matters.

Cheryl told her to go in.

Rex rose behind his desk when she entered.

From nervousness and at a loss for words, she said the tritest and most obvious: "Rex, you wanted to see me?"

"Yes, Lizbeth. Please sit."

She sat in the leather chair in front of his desk and rested her arms on the cold, plump armrests.

"Lizbeth, you know that I have always admired and highly respected you as a teacher. And I'm sure you're aware that I have liked you personally more than I should. I have often fantasized about you as my wife."

Lizbeth felt herself blush, sat silent, then said, "Yes, thank you, Rex, I've felt that and I'm flattered."

"I'm telling you the truth, Lizbeth."

She looked into her lap.

"Let me come to the point. Ralph Warner was here about half an hour ago."

Lizbeth looked up at him.

"He told me about your affair with his wife. He's vicious."

"He came to see me, too. Probably just before he came here."

"Lizbeth, what am I to do?"

She didn't answer.

"If this was Marydale when I was there, the headhunting redneck husband would have destroyed you by now."

He sat looking at the beautiful woman before him, her champagne blond head still bowed.

"May I ask you point-blank how serious this relationship is?"

135

Lizbeth met his eyes. Without a display of emotion, she said, "We love each other. He has divorce proceedings underway."

She paused. "Gillian moved in with me this week."

"That's another thing to think about. His suit might "out" you."

"I don't care, Rex. And if it does, I can handle it."

"What about your colleagues?"

"Rex, I can handle them, too."

"But...." He hesitated before he said, "Look at the way some of them treat Rutland's situation."

"He and Traci ignore it. If there are still some small minds on the faculty, Rex, it can't be helped. I think that my life style is accepted, as is a gay man's, more than inter-racial situations."

Rex recalled an incident at Marydale when he was Dean of English. One of his female faculty and a male teacher from another department who couldn't have children adopted two African American babies. They were ostracized and name-called so badly by their neighbors and some colleagues that they had to resign their positions, sell their home, and move away. They bought a farm in Nebraska; that was the last anyone, including their faculty friends, ever heard of them.

When he didn't respond, she said, "Funny, isn't it, Rex?"

While he was reminiscing, his eyes were trance-like. When he heard his name, his eyes flicked quizzically and refocused on her.

"All these years, you and I never interfered in each other's life. You never questioned me about my personal life. I've always respected you for that."

"Lizbeth, you have always been a very private person. I did, however, wonder why you wouldn't let me pick you up for the AIDS benefit."

"But Gillian wasn't with me then. It's just my way."

"Lizbeth, no one knows this, but I was married for quite a while. Lora was a beautiful blond, too. I guess I have an affinity for blonds."

He chuckled.

Lizbeth smiled understandingly, got up from her chair, leaned down and put her hands over his clasped ones on the desk. She looked intently into his eyes for a moment, withdrew her hands, then sat down again.

"We met in undergraduate school. We were very much in love. We married after commencement. She taught math and I worked on my graduate degrees. I'm not sure you're aware of the toll that working on degrees takes on a marriage when one works and the other is pursuing a higher degree. Papers, seminars, research for me. The brunt of everything fell on her. Correcting papers, doing lesson plans, cooking, cleaning, laundering on weekends, shopping for the week.

"Well, just before I received my master's in English, we had a long talk. No animosity. She decided that it would be better if we separated while I worked on my doctorate."

He unclasped his hands and leaned back in his chair, looking down at the desk and unconsciously rubbing his index finger along the edge as if he were dusting it.

"Well, while I worked on my Ph.D. at Maryland, I taught at Marydale—a two-year college—where I became Dean of English. Meanwhile, and finally, Lora wrote and asked for a divorce."

There was a great electric lull in the office.

He sat up and looked again at Lizbeth.

"You're the first woman I have ever thought of since."

He arose and came around the desk to her.

She stood.

They were close.

"May I kiss you?" Lizbeth asked.

Before he could answer, she put his large hands around her waist, her soft palms to his cheeks, and gave him a long, tender kiss on his lips.

When she drew away, with her hands still on his cheeks, she looked deep into his eyes.

"Rex," she said, "if I could love a man, you would be the man I would love."

"Thank you, Lizbeth."

She drew away and walked out of the office.

He saw her leave through blurred eyes and was only faintly aware of the soft click of the closing door.

* * * * *

"Marion, I'm happy you've come. You never forget me."

"Sometimes it seems to me that I do because I don't visit often enough."

"Can I get you something to drink? Rather, can you come with me and get yourself something to drink?"

Sarah smiled and chuckled softly deep in her throat.

"Maybe later. Let's catch up on things."

"As some tired comedians on TV would say, 'What's to catch up on?' Nothing ever happens. I told you about our trip to the city. That was the first thing in the year and the last thing since."

Sarah looked down at her hands folded in her lap.

Marion thought she saw a tear fall onto them. And another which missed her hands and dropped onto the burgundy skirt making a darker sanguine spot.

"Sarah, what's the matter?"

She got up from the wing chair opposite and went to her. She cradled Sarah's head against her.

Sarah sobbed harder, her head rocking against Marion.

"Tell me what's wrong," she said.

"It's Edward. When I ask him what's wrong, he says nothing, not even in defense of himself and his actions or the lack of them."

"What do you mean?"

Sarah pulled away from Marion and took a handkerchief from her skirt pocket. She wiped her eyes and blew her nose, then held it in her clenched hands in her lap.

Marion sat down again.

Sarah's head moved up and down, her eyes were closed, and her lips quivered and her voice cracked.

"Well, he stays up as late as possible when he's home just to avoid any physical contact with me. We've had separate bedrooms since my accident, but he hasn't been in mine for so long that I can't remember when he was in there last."

Marion didn't know how to act or react with someone who was confessing something so personal.

"When I say I'm going to bed, he kisses me on the top of my head as if I were a child. Often I'm still awake in the darkness when I hear him go to bed shortly after me. Sometimes I leave my light on hoping he'll just check on me and see if I'm all right."

Marion sat looking down at the wood grain pattern of the coffee table between them.

"He sometimes goes to his office at the college after dinner and works late. Most of the time, I never know how late because I fall asleep. Before my accident and while I was recuperating, he worked at the desk in his room." She blew her nose. "Oh, Marion, what could be wrong?"

"I understand that men his age often go through those stages. They withdraw and sort of live within themselves. They don't talk much. It's like they have something burdensome on their minds. Almost like the behavior of a woman in menopause."

"We're all about the same age. Did Gerald go through this?"

"No. But everyone is different. Not *all* men go through it. Then, again, Gerald might go through it later. Just like women. There's a variance in age. For men, it begins somewhere between forty-five and fifty-five."

"How long will this last?"

Marion shrugged her shoulders. "I've read that men go through it for about five years. It has something to do with some men's fear of encroaching age. It's a mental attitude, not the physical change that women go through."

Sarah had stopped crying and was listening intently.

"And it happens without warning?"

"What do you mean?"

"There are no signs beforehand?"

"No. It's not like the fire of hot flashes which we'll have to suffer when we start into menopause. Many women are also miserable to live with during that time, not really wanting to be or even being able to control their dispositions. It's a difficult time. They become fiercely jealous and imagine all sorts of ridiculous things and make life hell for their husbands."

"I can't remember my mother or father going through anything like that," Sarah said.

"My mother's disposition didn't change, but I remember how red she got and how she burst into a sweat and decried the curse of it." She shook her head as if to shake off the memory of her mother's inescapable and frequent discomfort.

"We have something to look forward to, don't we?" Then she said, "Marion, let's go to the kitchen. Lela made a sinful devil's food cake. You make the coffee or tea, whatever you want."

She put her hands on the arms of the chair and lifted herself. Leaning on her crutches, she took small steps toward the kitchen.

Marion followed her.

"I'd like a cup of good hot black coffee," she said, "and a great chunk of that sinful cake to go with it."

Sarah laughed aloud through the last sniffle, wiping her eyes and nose with her handkerchief before she slipped it into her skirt pocket.

They worked together preparing a midafternoon snack that they laughingly labeled a "caffeine binge to lift their spirits."

* * * * *

Driving home, Marion's mind wandered over a few incidents in the past. Last October, when she and Gerald were on their way to Traci and Rutland's for the celebration dinner, she thought she saw Edward driving toward them. Gerald didn't see him, because his eyes were on the road. Because she wasn't quite sure it was him, she didn't say anything to Gerald. And then, before that, the long Shakespeare weekend in early September which Sarah had asked about—the conference Gerald strangely enough had not known about. And Gerald's beautiful way of saying that he wouldn't have gone anyway, because he not only didn't teach Shakespeare but also because he didn't go to conferences.

I wonder, Marion thought.

PART III

A *Riddle* Solved

March, 1999

Chapter 8

THE FIRST TWO WEEKS OF MARCH were hectic for everyone—faculty and students alike. Mid-term exams had to be prepared and given before the break. For faculty being evaluated, student evaluations had to be taken in each class and then compiled by the secretaries; peer classroom visits and forms had to be completed. For the student, midterm break was a relief. For the professors, mid-term break meant correcting the examinations to be returned on the first day back.

Amid all of the hubbub, Stamford Blake of Crispin and Crispin took Gerald's manuscript with him.

* * * * *

Edward had given his last mid-term and was in the hallway turning the key in the lock of his office door.

"Hello, Professor Kendrick."

Edward turned. There were two students.

"Hello, Eric." On finally recognizing the other, he said, "Hello, Michael."

"I saw you in January with your daughter going into The Sand Dab," Eric said. "I called to you, but you didn't see me. She's quite a beauty. Real cool."

Edward blanched—he was sure—noticeably. He managed to stumble a thank you.

"I guess there's no chance for an introduction."

Edward laughed.

"Could be."

"I'll hold you to that."

Edward smiled and nodded.

As they moved away, Edward said, "Have a good break, guys."

"You, too," they said in unison.

He could hear Eric extolling his *daughter's* attributes to Michael as they walked down the hall.

Just as he was about to turn away from the door, Edward heard his office phone ring. He hadn't yet put his keys in his pocket, so he quickly unlocked the door and hurried to the phone. He didn't take the time to go around the desk; he leaned over it and snatched the handset.

"I was hoping I'd catch you before you left."

"I was just outside the door when the phone rang."

"What are your plans for the break?" Sheila asked.

"I have none really, except to correct papers."

"How dull. Could I liven things up for you sometime?"

"When?"

"My time is yours. I have nothing scheduled for the break except a trip to Capitola one day with my mom to spend the afternoon."

"How about Thursday afternoon about two?"

"I'll be waiting."

* * * * *

Most of the faculty spent a few days away during the break. Marion and Gerald spent three sun-filled days rediscovering Santa Barbara. Traci and Rutland drove to LA to spend a day at the Getty Museum and then returned north to Pismo Beach where they stayed for two days devouring Pismo clams. Lizbeth and Gillian spent lazy afternoons together having lunch at small Carmel and Pacific Grove bistros and then lying nude and making love poolside at Lizbeth's.

* * * * *

When Michael had a break during his shift just before two o'clock—he always had chilled salads prepared as an accompaniment for the regular entrées to which the waitresses could add the customer's choice of dressing from the stainless steel well containers in front of his salad bar—he called Sheila and said he'd like to see her this afternoon and then take her out to dinner.

"Michael, I'm sorry, I'm busy this afternoon."

"Then how about dinner?" he persisted.

"I don't think so, Michael."

"What is it with you? You came on to me and now I'm a quick shutoff. I don't understand."

"There's nothing to understand except that that phase of my life is over. It's something that happens to all of us."

"Then why hasn't it happened to me?"

"I don't know. Look, I've got to hang up now."

And she hung up.

Michael went back to finish his shift. There were a couple of grilled chicken salads and shrimp salads to prepare as well as restocking the regular house salads for the next shift.

Traffic was minimal going south on Route 1. He turned left onto the Valley Road.

His mind was whirling with Sheila. This was a blatant end. There had to be someone else. *I've got to know. She had to hang up right then. Who came? I'll drive past her place and see if anyone is still there.*

With his mind made up, he drove past the village and turned on Robles del Rio, crossed Rosie's Bridge, made a right, and climbed the tree-lined road.

A black Honda Accord was parked in front of the garage door.

There is someone. Who could it be? I'll find out if I have to stay here all night.

He looked at his watch. It was four-fifteen. Already more than two hours. He decided to drive up to The Ridge, park the car diagonally

145

against the rock wall, and walk back down. The density of the trees would give him ample cover; he would be able to see who came down the side steps.

What if he leaves while I'm parking?

He'd have to risk it.

Traffic this early and this high up was sparse because the dinner crowd had not yet begun to arrive.

Michael found a perfect vantage point down the sloping berm among the trees; if anyone came up the road, he wouldn't be seen, and he couldn't be noticed from Sheila's.

At five-thirty he heard voices coming from the garage area. On the deck above the steps leading to her apartment, he saw a man's back and Sheila's arms clasped around his neck. They must be kissing. They separated and Sheila—in her green robe—came to the edge of the deck as the man turned to descend the steps. On the gravel at the bottom—facing her—he blew a kiss upward; Sheila laughed and blew one back. As she yelled, "Soon," he nodded. After he disappeared out of Michael's sight, Michael heard the slam of the door, the whirring catch of the ignition, the slide of gravel under the tires, and the musical dum-diddy-um-dum of the horn.

Professor Kendrick.

His daughter, indeed!

PART IV

The *Cruelest* Month

April, 1999

Chapter 9

WHAT MORE APPROPRIATE WORDS for April than T. S. Eliot's, thought Gerald, as the lines went through his mind. *'April is the cruelest month, breeding/Lilacs out of the dead land, mixing/Memory and desire, stirring/Dull roots with spring rain.'*

He sat at his desk correcting themes, thinking about the outcome of the evaluation. He had an appointment with Jesse Keller at two o'clock. All evaluation materials had been collated by the three secretaries, and it was only the beginning of the second week of April.

He looked at his watch. One fifteen. He had time to get a bite of lunch in the cafeteria. Just as he stepped outside, Rutland came down the hall.

"I'm going to the cafeteria, Gerald. Join me?"

"That's where I'm headed. I have a two o'clock meeting with Keller. The evaluation."

"I have one with Starblack at three."

"Let's have a tall coke and make a toast," Gerald said.

* * * * *

"You can go in now, Gerald," Jo, the secretary, said.

Gerald opened the door.

Jesse was sorting through papers. He looked up.

"Gerald," he acknowledged with a nod. "Sit down."

Gerald sat in the chair in front of the desk. He crossed his legs, put his elbows on the armrests, and intertwined his fingers.

"Here." Jesse shoved the sheaf of multicolored papers beyond his blotter to the edge of the desk. "This is yours. Everything is there. The score sheet is on top, naturally. A copy has been filed."

Gerald leaned over and took the sheaf of papers. He looked at the score sheet and placed them in the attached manila envelope.

"Your student evaluations are great, as usual, and their written comments are excellent. There's no doubt that you *are* a good teacher."

"Thank you, Jesse. You know I love teaching."

"It shows. Your score with the students is the maximum of forty percent. It's the other areas in which you have failed to gain points."

"But isn't teaching the reason I'm here?"

"Absolutely, but the board wants additional extracurricular things from the faculty."

"Jesse, I don't believe in those conferences and conventions. There's so much self-aggrandizement in some of the speakers that it makes me sick."

"How about the department faculty colloquia once a month?"

"I'd rather not give my personal opinion, if you don't mind? That I don't attend them is obvious. Why? I'd rather not say."

"That's your prerogative."

Jesse cleared his throat and ran his hand through his thinning red hair. "I must turn in a score sheet to Rex, you know that."

"That's procedure."

"And I'll have to give my recommendation."

"Which will be?"

"Since you are evidently an excellent composition teacher, I will recommend that you continue to carry five composition courses as your course load each semester."

"That's fine with me. You're in charge."

"That's all, then."

Gerald rose and turned to go.

With his head bowed as he shuffled papers on his desk, Jesse said, "No, we can't give points for a work in progress. We must see the finished product between covers."

Then he looked up at Gerald and smirked, "By the way, how *is* the Great American Novel?"

Gerald glowered at him without answering.

In the long silence, Jesse kept shuffling papers without looking up.

"Jesse, I'd like to ask you something. What have I ever done to make you act with me the way you do? I think as two mature men, it's time we discuss it and stop ignoring or dodging the fact that something exists."

Jesse didn't answer.

"For some reason you have a dislike for me. Everyone notices the way you treat me."

He stopped shuffling papers and looked up.

"How do I treat you?"

"You're abrupt with me. If I want to talk with you in the hallway, you're too busy because you have a meeting to go to. At department meetings, you rarely acknowledge my hand when I want to contribute something. I don't discuss it with anyone because I really don't talk to many people, but they bring it up to me."

"I know you're a loner except for your friendship with Rutland."

"Is it my friendship with Rutland that has made you dislike me?"

Jesse sat back in his chair and twirled his pen in his fingertips.

"I may be many things and have many problems, but I am not a racist."

"I'm glad to hear that."

Gerald dropped the envelope on the seat of the chair as he moved behind it and stood gripping the back of it to face Jesse.

"Then what is it? I have no animosity toward you."

Jesse now sat forward and set the pen aside. He stretched his arms and folded his hands on the desk in front of him.

"I'll tell you because I know you're the gentleman I can't always be. Are you ready for this?"

Gerald nodded.

"You're the teacher I've never been or could ever be."

Gerald couldn't believe what he was hearing.

"Anyone can be an administrator. But I'm not even an administrator. I'm somewhere in between. I'll never go beyond this limbo. I don't even have to think. I just manipulate and make sure everyone teaches and that no one rocks the boat."

Gerald held up his hand to stop Jesse from continuing.

"Jesse, you're being too hard on yourself."

"Maybe I am, Gerald. Let me share something else with you. I don't want you to teach anything but composition, because you're the best on campus. You have no peer here. I realized that the one and only time I've ever seen you teach. That was when I first came here four years ago when you asked me to be your peer evaluator. Since then, students have further established that fact verbally to me as well as in writing on your evaluations."

"Jesse, you get evaluated."

"Yes, and I've never had a bad one from any of the composition faculty. That means, Gerald, that you have always given me a good rating, even though I've kept you from teaching in another department."

Gerald couldn't look at Jesse; he looked down at the manila packet on the chair seat.

"Jesse, I feel sorry for you."

"Why, Gerald?"

Now Gerald looked up and stared down at Jesse, eye to eye.

"As trite and as cliché as it is, I'll say it. Because of your professional jealousy, I can't believe that you would keep someone from expanding himself. You're supposed to be an educator, not an egoist building an empire. I could be as good in some areas of literature as I am in composition. You've seen my transcripts."

He picked up the packet from the chair and turned abruptly. He stopped with his hand on the knob and spoke to the closed door. "I forgive you, Jesse."

He closed the door soundlessly.

Gerald, I need you to continue to perpetuate the excellent rating of my department. You'll get the same superior recommendation you've always gotten. The board never sees the entire package. I'm in charge here, and what I say goes. All I do is send your name on my list to Rex. Because it's true. You are *excellent. You* are *the best. I've let you think I've been unfair, and you have every reason to hate me.*

But, Gerald, you don't have hate in you. I know that. And you know what? I hate me for what I've done to you all these years. I've been selfish in keeping you in my department because you are a real teacher and I didn't want to lose you. I've even been jealous of the respect and affection you have always gotten from the students, when I should really have felt only pride. Gerald, I'm the one who should be sorry for me, not you. I wish you could hear my inner voice. I want you, in your heart, to please forgive me.

* * * * *

The knock on the kitchen door was insistent. There were power and meaning behind it.

Sarah was awakened from her afternoon nap by the hardness of the sound; she looked at her digital clock on the bedside stand; it was four o'clock and Lela had gone.

Wondering who it could be, she shifted her legs from under the covers to the side of the bed, reached for her wine-colored velour robe which Lela had laid at the foot of the bed, and slipped into it. Holding onto her crutches, she steadied herself, then tried to gather enough strength to crutch-walk.

Heavy knocking again—more insistently.

Frustratedly—because she knew no one could hear her from where she was—she called out more for herself than to anyone else, "Just a minute. I'm coming."

As she maneuvered herself through the bedroom and into the hallway toward the back entrance, she shook her head in an effort to clear it. Edward had always told her not to answer the door when he or Lela weren't with her because she was at a disadvantage. Never mind. This was a rare occasion, and she was lonely to talk to someone. Just how lucid she would be because of the half sleeping pill she had taken less than a half hour ago, she couldn't tell.

"Professor Kendrick?" a throatily masculine voice called.

"Just a minute," Sarah called back to the voice as she neared the door.

Through the window she saw a strong square angry young face of about twenty. He was boyishly attractive with a mass of soft wavy hair and the classy sulky look of a young Leonardo DiCaprio.

153

"Professor Kendrick?"

"Just a minute," Sarah said again.

She reached the door and opened it.

"He's not here," she said.

"Oh? You were asleep?"

She half-nodded.

"I'm sorry to bother you."

"I'm Mrs. Kendrick," she said. "Can I help you?"

"I have a problem with Professor Kendrick that I wanted to discuss."

"He's delivering a paper at a conference in New Orleans, and I don't expect him until Sunday."

With a sense of finality to close the conversation and the door, she said, "You can see him in his office on Monday."

Hearing the tone of her voice, he took a step forward to keep the door from closing.

Then he said, "That's okay."

After another space of time, as his eyes went over her body, he said, "You'll do."

"What do you want?"

"It doesn't matter."

"I don't understand."

"Does it matter?"

Nervously, Sarah drew her robe tighter around herself. As she did so, she nearly lost balance while leaning on her crutches.

"Whoops! Here, let me help you."

"Thank you. I'm fine. I don't need help."

She attempted to brush his hand away.

"You do if you're alone."

"You can go now. What is your name? I'll tell Professor Kendrick you were here."

"That's not necessary."

He took another step forward, and, as he did so, Sarah tried to push the door closed, but he had all of the advantages and forced himself inside, holding her back gently with his hand and shutting the door behind him with his other.

Sarah felt the pulse of her heart like a great lump throbbing at the base of her throat—almost choking her.

When he reached for the crutches, she tried to pull away and, instead, reeled into a near topple. He grabbed her and held her close as the crutches clattered to the floor.

"I didn't know the great professor had such a good-looking wife."

"What do you want? Let me go."

His face was only inches from hers, and his arms crushed her tightly to his body. She felt his youthful, muscular leanness against her and the animal strength in his arms around her body. His breath was warm and sweet on her face. She tried to squirm out of his grasp but, with every effort, he held her tighter until he became aware of her nakedness under the robe.

"Mmmmmm," he murmured softly. "Wow. Let me see."

He moved her body away from his a matter of inches but still held her in a vise-like grip as he looked down at her full uptilted white breasts where the robe had parted slightly. He twisted her right arm behind her in a painful lock as he opened the sash. She tried to strike him with her other hand but, when she did, he twisted the arm behind her with such a wrench that her effort to hit him was foiled by the pain and her left hand fell limply to her side. He then grabbed her left hand and held it firmly so that she could not move. The robe slid all the way open. A smile crossed his face. His eyes crinkled with pleasure.

"God! What a beautiful body."

Sarah was whimpering now—softly and frightenedly.

"Leave me alone, please. Don't hurt me. Please. Please."

"I won't *hurt* you. I'll *please* you," he mocked.

He let loose of her hands and scooped her up in his arms. She wriggled violently, trying to free herself even if it meant that she might fall to the floor in a heap. At least there she might curl into a fetal position and avoid the inevitable.

But his grip was firm and he was uncannily strong. He held her right arm close to her body so that she couldn't swipe at his face. Her left arm was pressed against his chest; she was unable to move. She was frantic now and her half-sobs, half-moans were muffled by his eager lips crushing her mouth. She tried to move her head away from his, but he had her helplessly pinned in his arms.

He carried her past the living room down the hall. As he kissed her, his eyes searched the open doorways.

155

Sarah thought she would faint; she could barely breathe, and she heard her own heavy breath noisily inhaling-exhaling against his face.

"Ah, here we are," he said when he saw the thrown-back covers on the bed.

He stepped through a door to his left; his eyes swept the room. "Yeah," he confirmed for himself, "this is your room all right. He doesn't sleep here, does he?"

Sarah couldn't answer. She was hysterical. She cried as she twisted in his arms.

"Hey, don't do that. Don't fight me and everything will be all right. I just want to make you feel good. Now, then, we have to find *his* bedroom."

With that, he swung around and went back into the hallway. He turned left and went to the door just beyond the open door of the obviously unused guest room and found a typically masculine room with books on the bedside stand, a navy moiré robe carefully folded and laid at the foot of the bed, heavy mahogany furniture including a desk, brass lamps, a walnut clotheshorse for a man's clothes standing near the doorway to the bath.

"Yeah," he said, "This is where we'll do it. In his bed."

He lay her on the king-size bed.

She couldn't move from fear.

"I might just stay until Sunday."

Sarah drew her hand up to her mouth and screamed "No" into her clenched fist as he sat beside her on the edge of the bed and removed his Nikes. He stood up and removed his red plaid shirt and neatly arranged it on the arms of the clotheshorse. He turned to look at her as he opened his belt and undid the metal buttons on the fly of his jeans. He slid them down and stepped out of them, then folded them neatly and put them on the hanger. Change fell with a metallic clink out of his pocket onto the carpet. He looked at the coin spill rather stupidly for a second before he moved toward Sarah who had curled up fetally on the bed, the robe folded around and under her, her arms holding it tight across her breasts.

Sarah watched him come toward her; he was wearing mini-briefs which were distended by the bulky erection and which were too narrow to contain all of him in this state; his erection jutted out of his briefs toward his navel. He slipped them over his hips and stepped out of them, his penis thrusting its great firm length at her.

Here is Priapus, she thought. *Oh, my God! My God! My God!* She slid toward the middle of the bed away from him and cried aloud, whimpering as he moved toward her.

He knelt on the bed and crawled to her. She tried to move away, but he grabbed her arm. She swung out at him and in that instant he was able to unfold her body and throw himself onto her, pinning her down. She tried to fight him, but he held her arms down at her sides. He rubbed his body against hers and in that way opened her robe again. He moaned softly as he felt her warm flesh against his nakedness.

"Lie still," he said. "Enjoy it. *I* plan to. God! You're a good looking woman."

With her arms pinned to her sides, her head twitching from side to side, and her moans and cries fighting against his rapaciousness, she felt him kiss her breasts gently, his tongue ending teasingly at the tip of each nipple before his mouth went down toward her navel.

Without wanting to, she felt herself relax under his tenderness.

When he felt her tension leave, he let loose her pinned arms and moved his head down between her legs. He moaned ecstatically as he moved his face and let his tongue search out the warmest, moistest spot.

Sarah stopped crying.

"Don't hurt me, please."

He lifted his head and looked into her tear-stained, fear-stricken eyes.

"I won't. I want to give you pleasure, that's all. I bet Professor Kendrick can't give you the kind I can. But then, maybe he can, he's giving it to Sheila."

He arched her back off the bed and removed the robe so that she lay stark against the bed covering. He knelt over her and rubbed his hands along the sides of her body; his great cock lay heavily on her belly. He leaned down and licked her full breasts which slanted sideways; he fondled and cupped them gently as he kissed them with warm open lips. He felt her nipples harden as she gave a sharp intake of breath.

Oh, my God, Sarah thought. *Oh, my God.*

"Oh, my God." This time it was almost a prayer said aloud and he looked at her and stopped.

"Am I hurting you? Your legs?"

She shook her head.

He brushed her lips with his; she opened her mouth to him and gave him her tongue, embracing it with his own. He spread her legs and teased her with the tip of his penis. Then he felt between her legs and discovered moisture. His or hers, he wasn't sure. He inserted his finger and discovered that she was moist and waiting for him. Slowly he entered her, and she stretched full-length like an awakening lynx to receive all of his magnificent length. He filled her with himself.

"Let's take it slow," he said. "I want it to last."

She couldn't stop herself from saying, "So do I."

"Oh, you poor beautiful woman."

She turned her head and wept softly against her arm which was stretched over her head.

He covered her face with tender kisses.

And she met his mouth with hers.

* * * * *

He folded her robe around her and covered her nakedness. He felt shame for his actions, for causing her such anxiety and misery.

He lifted himself off the bed and, turning his back to her, dressed. "Forgive me," he said as he did so. "I'm so sorry. I'm not a rapist. I'm a nice guy. I don't know what got into me. I guess, for an angry, irrational minute, I wanted to take revenge on Professor Kendrick for sleeping with my girl and taking her away from me."

Fully dressed, he turned and looked at her. She was staring through the emptiness at the ceiling.

He sat on the edge of the bed.

Softly, he asked, "What's your name?"

She answered just as softly, "Sarah."

"Oh, you poor beautiful woman." He leaned on his elbow, ran his hand along her cheek, and brushed away fragments of tears which he wiped on his jeans. "He's a bastard for treating you like this."

She reached down and took his hand from his thigh. Pulling it toward her, she pressed her lips to his palm, then whispered, "Kiss me."

Leaning alongside her body, he turned her face to his, kissed away the remnants of tears on her closed eyelids, and gently touched her mouth with his.

She continued to lie with her eyes closed.

When he drew away from her, she thought she heard a pitiful, self-tortured sigh, and a whispered, "I'm so sorry."

She felt him rise from the bed and heard his soft tread on the carpeting. After a few minutes of silence, she heard him return. Then, again, "Forgive me. I'm so sorry." His voice trailed off.

When Sarah finally opened her eyes, lifted herself and leaned back on her elbows, he was gone. Her crutches were within her reach.

She lay back down.

"Don't be," she said, answering the echoes of his voice and footsteps in the empty room.

* * * * *

Late afternoon hall traffic was always light. The few afternoon classes were finished by four-thirty.

Edward sat facing the window as he worked on his computer, his back to his office door. The late afternoon sun pierced the Levolor shade and reflected thin slats of light on the ceiling which in turn cast silver shafts onto his desk.

"Professor Kendrick."

Edward was startled by the voice for a second but then more rattled by whose voice it was.

"Yes, Michael?"

Edward didn't turn around to face Michael; he kept his hands at the edge of the keyboard.

"I have something to tell you."

"Like what?"

"Like you've been fucking my girl."

Edward sat motionless, his eyes on the screen but not seeing the words on it.

159

"Nothing to say? Then listen to this. I fucked your beautiful lonely wife. On your bed."

There was silence for a moment as Michael let sink in what he had said.

The loose change on the floor near my bed when I returned from the conference in New Orleans. Oh, my God!

"I didn't want to hurt her. I wanted to hurt you. I hated myself afterward."

Edward could hear the sneer in Michael's voice as he said what he had. Then he heard a mocking chuckle.

"I told your wife about Sheila."

A pause.

"That's all I have to say. Oh, and one more thing, I told her you're a bastard for treating her the way you have. She needs love and deserves it. I could feel her loneliness. She shared it with me—not in words, but in actions."

Edward heard movement and assumed that Michael had left the doorway. He didn't swivel around to his desk.

He sat there for an interminable time as everything sank in; his shoulders shook with silent heavings, and sobs burst from his trembling lips. Tears dropped onto his lap.

How long had she known and said nothing! Oh, God, what must I have made her suffer? You're right, Michael, I am *a bastard.*

He took a handkerchief from his right hip pocket, left it unfolded, and wiped his eyes and cheeks.

He turned to his desk.

A sparkle of sunlight glistened briefly on the horns of the crystal satyr which Sheila had given him. He picked it up, held it a moment over the wastebasket, then set it on the desk in front of him.

From the top left drawer of his desk, he withdrew the blue velvet box containing the Austrian crystal Aphrodite which Sarah had given him when they returned from San Francisco. He lifted the hinged lid; a quick, sharp prism of sunlight hit the crystal and refracted into his face for a second. He took the goddess out of the box and placed her opposite of where he had had the other piece of crystal. As he set it down, he said through sobs, "Sarah, I'm so sorry."

He picked up the satyr which Sheila had given him, put it in the box, and closed the lid with a snap.

He dialed 9 for an outside line and then dialed Sheila's number. When she answered, he said, "I'm on my way."

"What a wonderful surprise. I can't wait."

He stood up and put the box in his herringbone tweed jacket pocket. He left his office without his attaché case.

* * * * *

Edward sped up Robles del Rio as fast as the winding road would permit. En route, his mind was as circuitous as the road. How to handle Sheila. How to face Sarah. How could he let himself get into such a predicament? How could he have treated Sarah as he had? And Michael? With Sarah! My God!

He turned onto the gravel driveway with more speed than he should have. When he came to a stop, he almost slid into the garage door. He did not bound up the steps as he usually did; he walked as a convict to his execution.

When he arrived at the landing, the door swung open and Sheila was there in her green robe. She locked her arms around him, her mouth turned up to him, but he didn't respond. She had sprayed her body with *Passion* for him.

When she realized his reaction to her, she stood back and knotted the belt of her robe more tightly.

"Something wrong?"

"Definitely."

Edward walked past her into the apartment, strode directly to the living room, and sat on the sofa.

Sheila closed the door and followed him.

For something to say, she asked, "Edward, can I get you a glass of wine?"

"It's *may*," he said irritably, "not *can*."

Then she said, "I'm *sorry*."

She stood in front of him.

"What's wrong?"

His elbows on his knees, he buried his head in his hands.

"God, Sheila, what have I done!"

"What *are* you talking about, Edward?"

She dropped to her knees in front of him and grasped his arms.

161

"Tell me, Edward."

He lifted his head from his hands. There were tears in his eyes.

"Michael came to my office this afternoon."

"Oh, my God, what did he want?"

Edward began to sob.

"He raped my wife."

Sheila gasped an "oh" and, covering her mouth, sat back on her legs. Her robe slid open, exposing her thighs.

Then she gasped aloud, "Oh, my God, Edward!"

"And he told Sarah about us."

She didn't say a word; she rocked off her legs onto the floor—her hands over her mouth.

Edward reached into his jacket pocket and retrieved the boxed crystal.

She looked at the blue velvet box, but didn't take it from him.

He opened it, withdrew the satyr, and stood it on the end table.

"What will we do?"

He took her face in his hand. He ran the fingers of his right hand through her long auburn hair and said, "It's over. Understand? We're finished."

She leaned further forward on her knees, grasping his hands to her breasts, and said with an hysterical note of panic, "No. Edward. We have to find a way to be together."

"Sheila, I can't leave Sarah."

"You love *me*, not her."

"No. Oh. No. Love was never meant to be in our relationship. That's why you gave me that satyr. Don't you remember?"

She pulled away.

"What do you mean?"

"Just what I said. I can't leave her. I've never told you I loved you because I love her!"

"Then I've been a plaything?"

"I'm afraid that's the way it has been."

"You sonofabitch."

"Don't say that. Sheila, we've had wonderful times together."

"I was your whore."

"No."

"Yes, Edward. You *used* me."

162

"What?"

He suddenly came awake to the moment.

"*I* used *you*? *You* seduced *me*!"

They were at loggerheads with their loud accusations.

Sheila covered her face with her hands and began to cry.

Edward reached out to her but, when she felt his touch, she pulled away from him.

"Go away! Leave me alone! You bastard!"

She sobbed into her hands

Edward stood up, touched her silken hair, and said, "I'll never forget you, Sheila."

"Go to hell!"

He hesitated a moment and then said, "I'm already there."

* * * * *

As Edward pulled into the driveway, he pressed the automatic garage door opener; the door slid up and he pulled inside. The next actions were done so quickly that they seemed to be done simultaneously: He turned off the engine, put the car in park, stepped on the handbrake, opened the door, got out, slammed the door, pressed the white button alongside the jamb, exited by the side door, heard the garage door slide down as he ran into the kitchen, slammed the door behind him.

"Sarah!" he called.

No answer.

"Sarah!"

He ran into the living room.

"I'm here," she called.

"Where?"

"In the den. I'll be right out."

When he heard her answer, he went back into the kitchen for a glass and for ice from the freezer. He returned to the living room and poured himself a scotch-on-the-rocks at the bar.

Sarah came out.

"You're home early."

He sipped from his drink.

Sarah crutched to her usual chair and sat.

Edward sat on the sofa and his glass rattled so that the ice-against-glass broke the silence.

"Sarah, I know."

She looked puzzled.

"What do you know, Edward?"

He looked into his glass.

"What happened to you."

"You've always known what happened to me."

"I don't mean that. I mean with Michael Larson, my student."

"Oh. Edward!" In shock, she put her hand to her mouth.

"Sarah, it's not your fault. It's mine! Oh, my God! "Forgive me. I did it to you, not him. I'm at fault for what I've been doing to you this past year."

"Edward, he told me you've been sleeping with his girl. Have you?"

He sipped his scotch.

"He told you the truth."

"Edward! Oh, Edward!"

Her face contorted as she broke into tears.

"Why did you neglect me?"

Now Edward broke into tears.

"Sarah, I'm so sorry."

She reached in her skirt pocket for a handkerchief.

She shook her head from side to side as she wiped away tears and blew her nose.

"How could you do this to me, Edward? You've hurt me so much that I can't tell you how much. I love you, Edward. Even now I still love you."

With his elbows rested on his knees, his head bowed in his hands, his hands buried in his hair, his body was racked as he sobbed uncontrollably.

"Not knowing why has been almost as bad as finding out. But the pain you've caused me, Edward! Why? I blamed myself and my lameness for your rejection of me."

His sobbing continued. Now he held his head in one hand and the crumpled handkerchief in the other, rubbing his eyes almost constantly.

"Edward, while you were cavorting with that girl, I had no one to talk to or confide in until I broke down one afternoon and mentioned it to Marion."

She was not crying now as she looked at him. She was growing strong and saying everything she needed to say.

"Marion thought you might be experiencing male menopause. How naive we were."

Her pain had converted to anger and her voice was almost a snarl.

"No, Edward, that wasn't it. It was infidelity. You had a young mistress. She must be less than half your age. For how long? More than a year. My grandmother used to say 'There's no fool like an old fool.' And, Edward, you *are* an old fool."

She wanted to lash out at him. Whip him with words. Flog him with thoughts. Bare his bones with memories.

"I suppose some of those conferences and trips were bogus, too. Was *she* with you?"

He still did not look at her.

He shook his head from side to side as he wept.

"*Was* she? That long weekend in San Francisco in September?"

"Don't, Sarah. Please!"

"Answer me, Edward. *Was* she?"

Edward groaned *"yes"* into his handkerchief, and his body shook.

Sarah said nothing for a long time; she just sat and watched him cry.

"Edward, I want to hurt you as you hurt me. The lonely nights I spent without you. The pat on the head you gave me as if you were pacifying a child. And the occasional kiss goodnight on the top of my head. Oh, Edward, how I wept."

She stopped for a minute, then said softly: "What a parallel. I'm like that Sarah in Capote's story 'Mojave' when she says: 'We all, sometimes, leave each other out there under the skies, and we never understand why.'" Her voice broke, but she quickly regained control of her emotions. "Now it's your turn. Cry, Edward. Try to wash away your guilt. I don't think you can, Edward. There aren't enough tears for all the injustice you perpetrated on me. And if there are, there will be *bloody* stains."

She stopped when her voice broke, and she wept fiercely, lifting her tear-stained face, letting the tears roll down her cheeks and drop off her chin onto her lap. She felt like Medea begging the gods to chastise Jason.

One more thrust, she thought, *to match the pain I've suffered.*

Her voice was barely more than a whisper when she said: "He didn't rape me, Edward. I welcomed it. It was beautiful."

The noise they heard was the movement of motes in the stillness of the room.

He looked up at her with red eyes.

His voice was a monotone.

"Oh, no. Don't tell me that, Sarah. Please don't."

"It's true."

He left the sofa and knelt in front of her, then leaned back on his calves.

Their eyes were level with each other. She looked directly into his.

"When he left, he apologized and said he was angry about you at first, but he made gentle love to me. He told me I was beautiful. Do you know how that made me feel after all the months you'd ignored me?"

With his eyes closed, he whimpered like a pain-ridden child.

"Of course you don't. I bet you told your little girl she was beautiful."

He shook his head.

As he said the word "Never," tears dripped from his open lips onto his chin.

"I'm sure you made wild love. Edward, what a fool you are for risking your career with a student." Then, sarcastically, she added, "I hope, for your sake, she was worth it."

Now he wiped his red eyes and opened them.

Sarah thought: *How pitiful you look, Edward. You should see yourself. If you could, you'd know what my eyes and heart have looked like for more than a year! Cry, Edward, cry more.*

"She seduced me, Sarah. Believe me."

"And the apple was there, so you took a bite."

He shook his head.

"Where did you go? To a motel?"

"No. To her place up Robles del Rio."

"What about her parents?"

166

"They live in Monterey."

"How convenient for you."

"Often?"

"Often what?"

"Did you have sex with her often?"

"Yes."

Sarah broke down again.

He moved forward and wrapped his arms around her. He put her head on his shoulder.

She let him.

"Oh, Sarah, it's all over. I told her today after Michael came to see me. It will never happen again. You're right. I *am* a fool. I love you."

He kissed her neck.

She forced her arm up between their bodies and wiped her eyes and nose.

"Edward, I love you, too."

She held his tear-wet face between her hands, looked longingly into his swollen eyes, and kissed him tenderly.

He responded as gently.

With her eyes closed and moist lips pressed to his, she said, "Edward, you've come back to me."

They kissed long—their lips trembling with salty tears that said more than words ever could.

* * * * *

Michael left the restaurant at the end of his shift and drove out Route 68 to Tarpy's where he was to meet Sheila. She had called him at the restaurant and asked him to meet her there after work.

He pulled into the parking lot near the entrance beside her black Spyder. In the courtyard, a few tables were occupied this late in the day, but she wasn't there. He went inside—slightly blinded from the white late afternoon sunlight—and, while he was being greeted by the hostess, he saw a blurred Sheila waving to his right from the center of the restaurant. She was the only person in that enclosed section, seated at the middle table against the stone wall between the muted earth-tone pastels of two caballeros.

"Hi."

167

He sat down, his back to the entrance.

"Hi. What's up?"

The red-haired waitress came and he ordered a Pacifico.

"Michael, what have you done?"

"What are you talking about?"

"You raped Professor Kendrick's wife."

"I did not."

"He told me today."

Flatly, he said, "He's been having sex with you."

"What?"

"I saw him leave your place after five one day."

"You were spying on me?"

The waitress brought his beer.

"I'll have 'nother short screwdriver. Short on juice 'n' ice, heavy on vodka," Sheila said.

"Right away," the waitress said as she took away Sheila's empty glass.

Michael squeezed the wedge of lime, dropped it into the glass, and took a sip of his beer.

"You remember the day I called you at two o'clock and you said you had to hang up? That was the day I drove out to your place after work. I parked at The Ridge, walked back down, and hid in the trees. It was five-thirty when Professor Kendrick came out. You were in your green robe, hanging all over him."

He took another sip of beer and licked the foam from his lips. He sat with his back against the wall.

Sheila stared at him but said nothing.

"I was shocked. He's more than twice your age. He should be ashamed of himself for taking advantage of you."

"But he didn't. I went after him. And I got him. At first it was just sex, but then I fell in love with him."

"Come on, Sheila, you've had psychology one-o-one. That's just a father fixation that passes. One of the examples given in psych was that female students often fall in love with their high school teachers or their college professors. They're just crushes which pass."

The waitress brought her screwdriver.

Sheila didn't acknowledge her.

"Well, mine didn't."

"Does he love you?"

She didn't answer.

Instead, she sipped her drink and smirked into it as she twirled it.

"What's that supposed to mean?"

"Was she as good a fuck as I am?"

He held off answering for a minute, then said, "She's a beautiful lady which I hope you will grow into one day."

"Ha!"

"He's a bastard for what he's been doing to her. He's been screwing you and God knows what else he's doing or *who* else. And leaving that lovely woman to suffer hungrily for him. She loves him."

"But she liked yours better. After all, it *is* enormous."

Ignoring her comment, he took another sip of his beer.

"Sheila, I love you. I know now that I loved you from our first time together."

She twirled her glass again, nearly spilling it, and salaciously looked up from under her eyelids at him.

"I never loved you, Michael. I was in love with your big cock. I love sex, and it was great with you. But, now I know there's more than *just* sex."

"Good. You're feeling something like I feel. But for you it's getting returned. Wait until it isn't. Then you'll know an ache."

He took a couple of swallows of his beer which was getting warm.

"He must be great."

"He is."

"What about his wife?"

"What about her? He'll leave her, I guess."

"That bastard. He doesn't know what he has."

"But she's crippled."

Michael was stunned. He sat upright in his seat and stared at her. "Oh, my God," he barely whispered, "how cruel you are. This is a side of you I've never seen. How could I ever have thought that I loved you?"

"There's a lot about me you don't know."

She looked at him with a smirk and emptied her glass, the ice clinking noisily as she lifted it high and drained it. Looking toward the bar, she summoned the waitress to bring her another.

"Sheila, you're driving."

"So? Fuck you! Why should you worry about me?"

"I care about other people."

"Cool."

"I'm glad you called me. This has been a real eye opener."

The waitress brought her drink.

"Would you like another beer?"

Michael looked up at her, smiled, and shook his head.

"So, what's he going to do? Leave her for you?"

"We haven't talked about that yet."

"A man you're having sex with tells you that I raped his wife and says nothing to you about the relationship between the two of you? Come on, Sheila, I'm a man. I know how a man thinks."

She stared a killer look at him.

"*Do* you?" she said. "Well, he's a different kind of man than you. You have to grow up."

She downed half of the screwdriver.

He was momentarily stunned by her remark. He retaliated. "And I know nice women, and you're not one. And psych one-o-one helped *me* a great deal. Evidently, it went over your head. He's not going anywhere with you. That's why you called me and that's why you're getting drunk. You can't handle it."

She finished her drink and stood up.

"Fuck you, Michael!"

She spat the words at him through gritted teeth, loud enough for the passing hostess to hear. Michael saw her turn her head and then turn away quickly.

As Sheila half-ran out of the restaurant, Michael detected a stagger. He knew she would be going out Route 68 and crossing the five miles of treacherous winding Laureles Grade because that was the closest way home.

He stood, reached into his pocket for his money clip, quickly peeled off a ten and a twenty, set his glass on top of them, jammed the clip into his pocket, and fled after her.

There was no traffic coming either way. His tires squealed as he burned rubber getting out of the parking lot. He saw the traffic light turn green at Del Ray Canyon junction; the line of cars began to slide slowly through it before they accelerated.

Damn! She's nowhere in sight. That crazy girl. She's crazy! She'll kill herself and maybe worse take someone else with her.

I love her. I've got to find a way to get her back.

I'll follow her home. I'll break down the door if she doesn't let me in.

But she's drunk and irrational. I won't be able to talk to her. All right, I'll just see that she gets home okay. Then I'll go up tomorrow after work and talk to her. Tell her I love her. Not tell *her!* Convince *her!*

Damn!

He was near the Laguna Seca entrance; there was a long string of cars stopped at the Laureles Grade turnoff.

* * * * *

Gerald called Marion and told her that he was going to Borders in Sand City after his office hours at two o'clock to pick up a book which they called to tell him had arrived. The clerk said that she would hold it for him, but he said that he really wanted to pick it up immediately, so he would be there shortly.

On his way home from Borders, as he waited for the red light to change on Route 68 before he could turn right onto Laureles Grade, he wished that he had ordered the book at The Thunderbird Bookstore in The Barnyard where he always dealt; however, he had been to the dry cleaner in Seaside and found it convenient at that time to go to Borders.

He shrugged his shoulders at the thought and mentally said, '*Oh, well*' as he started up the Grade; the few cars which had turned were quite far ahead and there was nothing behind him. Going up the Grade from Route 68 was a less steep and winding climb than coming from the valley on the other side. At the top where the marker indicated the summit at 1284 feet, he started down a slight incline; the view across the canyons was breathtaking and he always drove more slowly here to enjoy it. He recalled the snow on the tops of the distant ranges last winter, and then the green spread after the generous spring rains.

Coming up from the valley, there were a few sharp turns that always made him apply a little brake, but he was at those turns right

171

now and going down didn't seem as treacherous. As he started down, he saw a fog bank to his right twelve miles away over the Pacific.

Winding down the Grade at forty-five miles an hour, he was suddenly aware of a black Fiat Spyder behind him, a young girl at the wheel, auburn hair streaming behind her in the wind, sunglasses as big as those plastic Solo salad dishes Marion bought at Safeway. She was blinking her lights at him.

Probably trying to tell me to go faster or to pull over.

He smiled into the mirror.

Impatient youth, rushing through life, not taking the time to see and enjoy the beauty around them.

He decided he'd pull off at the second to last curve before the straightaway, where he could glimpse the first full view of the valley which he loved so much.

She was still blinking her lights and tailgating him.

The second-to-final turn was just ahead.

He rounded the curve, turned his wheels as they touched the dirt and gravel of the turnoff, and put his foot on the brakes.

They locked.

The Spyder honked its horn, waved its hand high in the air, wove around the final curve, and sped down to the valley floor.

Chapter 10

REX LIFTED THE BRASS KNOCKER and touched the back plate gently. In a few moments, Traci opened the door.

"I didn't know whose car that was, but I sighed relief when I realized someone was with Marion. How is she?"

"She's in her bedroom. Rutland is with her. She's in shock, Rex. All she does is say Gerald's name over and over. We've called our doctor, Bill Mason. He should be here shortly to give her a sedative."

"How did it happen?"

Traci told him what she knew.

"One of our students, Michael Larson with a cell phone, saw the wrecked car in the turnoff on Laureles Grade and called the highway patrol. They called the emergency ambulance patrol in the valley. When they arrived at the scene, he was dead. His brakes locked and he slid sideways across the turnout, hit and buckled a fence which checked the velocity, then hit a tree which stopped the car from careening over the canyon. He died instantly from a broken neck."

She broke into quiet sobs, and Rex held her close. When her shaking finally subsided, she continued to give him the details in a nonstop flat staccato.

"The ambulance took Gerald to the hospital. He was pronounced dead on arrival. Another highway patrol car came to the house and told Marion the news. They took her to the hospital to identify Gerald's body. They wanted to administer a sedative, but she refused. What they thought was calmness was shock. They should have given her one regardless. The highway patrol car brought her home. She gave them my name to call. They wouldn't leave until we arrived. We've been with her all night. She went in and out of sleep, but when the realization hit her this morning she lapsed into shock. That's when we called our doctor. After that, we called Jesse Keller at home and told him to cancel Gerald's classes and to call you. We also told him not to say anything to anyone until you made decisions."

They heard a car pull into the driveway. A door slammed. Traci opened the front door for Bill and led him into the bedroom. He opened his bag on the way and set it on the bed; he tore open a foil-covered alcohol pad, wiped Marion's arm, withdrew a vial from his black valise, tore off a paper protector from the needle, filled it, then jabbed it into her upper arm. Within minutes, they saw her body go slack.

"She'll be fine for a few hours," Bill said.

They left the bedroom and closed the door.

"Why don't the two of you go home and get some sleep. I'll stay here with Marion," Rex said.

"There's nothing anyone can do for her now," Bill said. He looked at Rex. "I'll give you sedatives for her." He set his bag on the sofa and withdrew a labeled plastic prescription container of Valium and handed it to Rex.

"If she's too anxious when the sedative wears off, give her a half. Then give her one before bedtime and one in the morning. Is there anyone we can call to stay with her?"

"There is no family, if that's what you mean," Traci said. "How about the Visiting Nurses Association?"

"I'll call," Rex said.

Bill went toward the door.

"Call me if you need me. And, by all means, have the nurse call me. She'll need twenty-four hour care for a while."

They thanked him and assured him they'd take care of matters.

Rex urged Traci and Rutland to go home. He said he'd call their departments and have their classes canceled.

He then called his secretary.

"Cheryl," he said, "call the president and tell him that Gerald Ritchey died in an automobile accident."

"Oh, no!" she gasped into the phone.

He then said, "And notify our people."

* * * * *

"So, you're a celebrity," Sheila said as she opened the door.

"A celebrity? How?"

"You found Professor Ritchey's car."

"I don't think that makes me a celebrity."

"Well, you made the *Herald* and TV."

"Can I come in?"

"And it's 'may' not 'can.' Sure. But why?"

He stepped over the threshold into the kitchen and stood there feeling awkward.

As Sheila closed the door, she told him to sit.

Michael pulled out a chair from the small table, maneuvered it askew, sat, and crossed his right leg over his left knee. His arm fell at an angle over the back of the chair. His chin rested on his chest. When Sheila didn't speak as she went to the sink board for coffee, he rocked his leg and foot as if to shatter the thick air in the room.

With her back to him, she said, "Coffee?"

"No. I've had two cups."

She shuffled in her slippers to the table and sat across from him. He didn't change his body position; he only lifted his head.

"No work today?"

"I took the day off. I'm still shaken after seeing the accident."

"Why? Did you know him?"

"No?"

"Well, then...."

"Sheila, what's wrong with you? A good man is dead in a freak accident."

"All I'm saying is that it has nothing to do with you...or me."

"Everyone is affected in some way or another. Anyone who reads a paper or watches TV."

"Doesn't bother me." She singsonged and lightly trilled the *me*.

Michael took a deep breath with his mouth open, puffed his cheeks and exhaled exasperatedly as he again dropped his head onto his chest.

Sheila put her elbows on the table; holding her cup between both hands, she blew into it before taking small sips of the steaming brew.

A few quiet moments passed.

"So, why are you here? To make me feel sorry about a man I didn't even know?"

Michael lifted his head and turned his chair into the table so he could face her.

"I followed you immediately when you left Tarpy's. I was worried about you because you were drunk and—"

She interrupted belligerently. "I *wasn't* drunk."

Then, looking into her cup, she sipped her coffee.

"—and because it was the beginning of rush hour and traffic was heavy on Sixty-Eight going east. I couldn't have been more than fifteen minutes behind you up the Grade. You must have seen Professor Ritchey's car ahead of you. And if it had already been wrecked when you went by, I'm sure you would have stopped."

"I'm not so sure I would have. I had other things on my mind as I was driving."

Michael looked down at his hands folded in the air between his legs and shook his head as if to clear it.

"You asked me why I'm here. I'm here because I love you. When I'm not with you, I miss you. I'm jealous when I see you talking to anyone else. I can't imagine you in a relationship with a man old enough to be your father."

Sheila set her cup down with a thump and leaned back in her chair. She threw her head back and laughed and laughed and laughed until she had to wipe away tears with the backs of both hands.

"What's so funny?"

"Me?" She pointed at herself. "You?" She pointed at him. "Oh, Michael. That's hilarious. After Edward? You're like a little boy."

Furious, Michael got up and moved toward her. He stood looking down at her upturned face which was still in the broad smile mode. "Say that again and I'll slap you so hard...."

In a soft emotionless voice, with crinkled eyes staring him down, she growled, "I dare you."

After a prolonged silence with his hand raised to slap her, he dropped it and walked to the window over the sink. Looking out through the oaks at the hills opposite, he said, "I told you at Tarpy's that I loved you and probably had loved you since the first time we met. We've known each other more than a year. We've made love a number of times."

"Not love, Michael. We had *wild, hot* sex."

"You were the first woman I ever had."

"You *are* a virgin? Then I taught you well. Edward's wife got the benefit of my teaching, though. Was she able to give you any extra pointers? I doubt it. She's been out of practice."

"You *are* a bitch."

"Because I'm calling the shots."

"She's a lady...."

"Ladies don't fuck?"

"I hate myself for...."

"Fucking a crippled woman? She was probably grateful. Edward didn't. I know that."

His resounding slap across her mouth sent her chair backwards. She landed on the floor in a scramble of legs and arms. Her green robe fell open to expose her nakedness, and her froufrou slippers flew across the room.

"You sonofabitch! You sonofabitch! Get out!"

"I'm not getting out."

"Why? Do you want to rape *me*, too?"

"You don't rape. You give it away."

"You men think you're the conquerors. We're the ones who manipulate. Yeah. That hot little thing between our legs does the manipulation, Michael!"

His voice was a soft monotone, when he said, "How could I ever think I loved you. The more I'm with you, the more I see other sides of you."

"They've always been there."

"Have you shown them to your dear professor."

"Just the other day."

"What was his reaction?"

"He walked out."

Michael chuckled. "The great love of your life. He was going to give up his wife for you."

"I'm glad he's gone. The sonofabitch."

"Suddenly everyone who rejects you is a sonofabitch."

"That's right!" She snarled the words between clenched teeth.

She scrambled onto all fours and nearly toppled as she stood screaming at him through strands of tousled auburn hair. Gesticulating with her arms like someone brandishing swords, she shouted: "I don't want to see him—or you—anymore! I hate both of you! I hate this Valley! I hate Valley Villa College!"

He grabbed her flailing arms and pinned them tight against his chest. Between clamped teeth, his lips curled, he half breathed, half snarled: "You hate yourself."

She spat in his face.

He pushed her away and wiped his face on his sleeve.

She lost her balance momentarily. When she regained her stance, she buried her face in her hands.

"I'm glad I found out who you are before it was too late. You're not worth loving."

He strode across the kitchen, nearly wrenched the knob out of the door, and slammed it behind himself. As he walked to the stairs, he ducked at the sound of shattered glass from the kitchen door. A small round object rolled down the steps in front of him; he couldn't discern what it was. Before descending, he turned and saw a small crystal statue of a beheaded satyr on the landing.

* * * * *

The California Republic flag in the college courtyard was lowered to half mast for a week.

* * * * *

Rex arranged for the nurses to visit on three eight-hour shifts. The week after the accident, as painful as it was, Rex had to broach affairs which needed to be discussed.

"Bless you, Rex, I understand."

He inquired into the disposition of Gerald's remains. Marion told him that she and Gerald talked of cremation and of having the executor of their will, whoever it might be, mingle their ashes before spreading them over the Pacific. Rex drove Marion to a crematorium in Pacific Grove to sign papers so that Gerald's body could be released from Community Hospital. While they were at the crematorium, Rex asked if she wanted to choose an urn for Gerald.

"Not right now," she said.

He visited Marion every afternoon. Traci and Rutland visited in the evening. After a week, Marion felt that she didn't need an evening nurse from three to eleven. When she did that, either Traci brought dinner or Marion cooked for the three of them.

Rex also took care of the insurance issues. The car had been towed to the Ford dealer in Seaside and the AAA adjustor declared it totaled. Marion did not want another car at the moment. The life insurance agent came to the house; Rex and Marion filled out the necessary papers and gave him one of the ten copies of Gerald's death certificate. Rex worked with personnel and handled the college insurance which paid Marion one-half of Gerald's one-year salary for the duration of her life.

* * * * *

The Student Government Association (SGA) collected enough money through the one-page *extra* edition of *The Villa*—the college paper—distributed campus-wide about Gerald's accident in order to afford their proposed memorial: a ten-foot cross of white roses at the site of Gerald's accident on the second-to-last curve on Laureles Grade. There were quotes in the college newspaper from Gerald's current students as well as from upper-class students who had had him as a freshman composition professor. The *Monterey Herald* story of the accident and of the SGA's tribute brought hand-delivered checks and cash to the SGA office on campus.

179

On the day of the rose memorial, the highway patrol blocked off both east and west traffic on the Grade between two and three o'clock. All of the local TV stations and *The Herald* notified the public of the brief stoppage.

Harry Seldridge, president of the SGA, had the rose cross erected against a backdrop of vibrantly yellow genista before anyone's arrival.

Cars lined Laureles Grade before and after the accident site, and everyone walked either up or down to the memorial service.

Rex, Traci, Rutland, Lizbeth, Edward, and Keller accompanied Marion. As they walked through the gathering crowd, Thamin, the maître d' from The Covey, stepped forward.

"Oh, my, Thamin. How good of you to come."

Marion extended her hand.

Thamin held it as he said, "Mrs. Ritchey, you have my deepest sympathy and my staff extends the same."

"Thank you, Thamin."

Thamin kissed her on the cheek.

She smiled and took her hand away. They proceeded toward the front row before the dais.

"Mrs. Ritchey."

Marion stopped and turned to see a lean, blond-haired young man dressed in black jeans and a black shirt step from the crowd behind her.

"Mrs. Ritchey, my name is Michael Larson."

Marion looked up at Rex beside her, somewhat nonplussed.

"He's the young man who found Gerald's car," Rex said.

"I'm so sorry. How could I forget your name?" Marion reached for Michael's hand and held it between both of hers.

"That's all right, Mrs. Ritchey. I understand. I just want you to know how very sorry I am about what happened. I only wish I had been there sooner."

"I'm happy you were there when you were. Thank you for what you did."

Looking around and gesticulating with his head, Michael said, "Sure are lots of people. He must have been a great man."

"He was a great man to many people. The greatest for me, Michael. He'll always be my love."

180

She dropped his hand and hugged him, gave him a kiss on the cheek, and then moved on with Rex.

The president, vice president, various deans of the college and Father Haggerty of Our Lady of Mt. Carmel Church had driven up earlier and were already milling around near the front row. As Marion passed them, they shook her hand and extended their condolences.

This was the first time that Marion had seen the site of the accident; she gasped audibly and turned away when she saw the freshly installed section of new fence behind the white rose cross.

Rex held her in his arms; she buried her face in her hands on his chest for a few moments until she regained composure.

Harry Seldridge extended his condolence to Marion, greeted Rex and the entourage of faculty whom he knew, then ushered them to their fold-out chairs before the cross.

Seated behind Marion were the entire English faculty and secretaries, and faculty from other departments.

Standing on the dais, Harry seemed to be dwarfed by the white rose cross and embraced by its extended white arms. A PA system had been set up and he held a microphone. The assemblage was quiet. The rest of the SGA cabinet stood on either side of him. From the dais, he could see the reporter and the cameraman from the *Herald* and the crew from *KSBW* standing on the road.

"Good afternoon, Mrs. Ritchey, President Wilson, Vice-President Merkert, deans of the college, Father Haggerty, faculty, personnel staff, fellow students, and friends.

"I am Harry Seldridge, president of Valley Villa Student Government Association, and I thank you for coming to our memorial service for Professor Ritchey. I want to thank all of you here and all of those who could not be here for the contributions for the rose tribute you see here. Because everyone who knew Professor Ritchey contributed so generously, we have been able to establish a generous trust fund for entering students at Valley Villa. It will be called The Gerald Ritchey Fund and will provide help for five students a year."

A warm, appreciative murmur ran through the crowd.

"I never had Professor Ritchey for a class, but a number of my friends had that distinct and fortunate pleasure. They told me more than once that, if it wasn't for his patience, his knowledge about writing, his thoroughness, his pleasure when he saw a student

181

succeed, and his love for his work, they would never have made it through their freshman year. Some of my friends are already in the business world and they've told me that they are doing well in their positions and allege that their success is due to what Professor Ritchey had taught them.

"As young as we are, we all have poignant memories of people who have influenced our lives, and, as we mature, I'm not sure that even an eternity will be enough time to recount them.

"I remember something told to the class by Professor Rostrand in British lit. We had just finished reading Virginia Woolf's *Mrs. Dalloway* and were discussing it philosophically. She told us that as long as we live on in others' memories, we are not gone. She gave herself as an example. She said that if she mentioned something beautiful and special that touched us to the core and we remembered it and told it to our children as it had been told to us by her, and they to their children, that she would live on to other generations.

"Well, that's what Professor Ritchey has done for all of those whose lives he's touched."

Harry could see handkerchiefs dabbing at eyes. Marion, in front of him, sat momentarily tearless and smiling, listening to his words and seeing the innocent beauty of white roses behind him.

"Among us, this afternoon, are people who would like to celebrate the man they knew. The first is Professor Rutland Jackson."

Rutland left his seat, stepped up onto the dais, and opened his manila folder at the lectern.

He began: "I've come to honor Gerald Ritchey as a fine professor and the dearest friend I've ever had. Gerald was my mentor when I came to Valley Villa and he has remained my closest friend and colleague these three years.

"As the president of SGA inferred, he was a teacher's teacher, as Hawthorne was a writer's writer. Gerald was as thrilled as the student, when a student went from nothing to something. In some cases, no one had really taught that student anything about good writing. But he sped them to the level where they should have been when they arrived in his class. It was a revelation for those students, and they loved him. They came back to him when they went on to upper-level courses and told him when they received A's on their papers. He glowed with pride for *their* achievements, not *his.*

"Wouldn't it be great if all of us wore such laurels and remained as humble, loving, and dedicated as he?"

Not one face in the audience averted his eyes which swept over them.

Rutland looked down at Marion.

With a quaver in his voice which made him hesitate long enough to clear his throat, he concluded: "Marion, my tribute to Gerald as a sensitive man, a true and devoted friend, and a dedicated teacher will never end as long as I live."

When he stepped down, he bent over and lifted her, then hugged her close and kissed her before he went to his seat.

Harry Seldridge introduced Jesse Keller. Although he went to the dais without a prepared speech, he gripped the sides of the lectern as if he was losing his balance.

"Marion," he began, looking down at her, "the students and the composition department have lost one of the finest teachers in the college.

"The first time I visited Gerald's class as a peer, I witnessed an unbelievable session. If the students hadn't had desks, they would have sat at his feet and been as mesmerized as the students at the feet of Socrates at the Academy. Gerald introduced me as the Chair of Composition. They weren't awed by my presence. As a matter of fact, when class began, I was a nonentity. I could tell by their questions that he taught passionately in every session. They were so attentive that they hung onto his every word. Not once did he sit at his desk. He walked among them asking questions. I could see that they had read the materials. When the class ended, they actually groaned."

There was a ripple of laughter at this.

He paused and smiled.

"They surrounded him at the lectern. Neither they nor Gerald saw me leave. That was an experience I have never forgotten.

"I only wish I had been such a teacher.

"There *is* a difference between a professor and a teacher. I have had professors who profess to teach and don't. But a *real* teacher is a rarity.

"Let me close now by saying this: Gerald Ritchey was a born teacher and *became* a professor. We, and all of his students, can thank God for that."

As Jesse stepped down, Marion arose.

He hugged and kissed her. Tears rolled down her cheeks. She wiped them, but they kept coming.

Jesse held her until he felt her body slacken. When she finally let go, he smiled at her through falling tears.

He simply nodded.

Their arms and hands lingered in parting.

Unashamed, Jesse stood erect, tears streaming down his face, and walked to his seat.

Harry introduced Father Haggerty to the assemblage.

Father stood before them in a black cassock; he was over six feet tall and seemed to tower as high as the cross in front of Marion.

He looked down at her benevolently.

A light wind stirred the folds of his white lace surplice and his glistening black hair which framed his large square face and cascaded to his broad shoulders.

Everyone was quiet.

"Mrs. Ritchey and friends," he began, "we're here to celebrate the wonderful unselfish life of the loved professor who devoted himself to the teaching of his students. I didn't know him personally, but many of the young people in my Carmel Valley parish have come to me for help because they have been totally shattered by the loss of this man who touched their hearts and expanded their minds.

"It's difficult for young people to think of death, and when the reality of it strikes them, they can only ask 'why'? 'Why him?' All of them who have come to me have not yet experienced a personal loss in their families—something which might have helped them to cope now."

He opened his psalm book. "Please let me share this Roman Catholic version of the twenty third Psalm with you."

Over the bowed heads, he read, "The Lord is my shepherd; I shall not want. In verdant pastures he gives me repose; beside restful waters he leads me; he refreshes my soul.... Even though I walk in the dark valley I fear no evil; for you are at my side.... And I shall dwell in the house of the Lord for years to come."

Father heard muffled sobs; he closed the psalm book, held it flat against his chest, and kept his head bowed in deep respect as he said,

"I'd like all of you, in silent prayer, to give thanks for having been able to share whatever time you had with Professor Ritchey."

The front row of college executives stood.

Marion sat.

All heads were bowed as Father gave a broad blessing to the gathered throng.

When the moment was over, Father Haggerty stepped down.

Harry spoke to the crowd.

"The state police were graciously cooperative to hold traffic for this hour, and I know we're all appreciative. Would you please make a pathway so that Mrs. Ritchey and her friends can leave first. Thank you."

Marion walked to the dais and Harry stepped down.

"Bless you. That was beautiful. Thank you."

She took his hand, and placed her other one on his cheek as she stood on tiptoe to kiss him. He bent down to accept it and saw Marion's wet-stained eyes.

Not a sound was heard and no one moved as Marion passed, head down, through the crowd.

Epilogue

May to November, 1999

Chapter 11

REX LOOKED UP FROM HIS DESK when he heard the knock on his door before it opened. Cheryl held a thick manila packet in her hand. "It's here," she said, and handed it to him.

"Good. Thank you."

He opened the packet and laid it on his desk. It was the usual compiled evaluation-results package from the faculty and chairs sent to him by President Wilson in advance of their combined conference; he thumbed through it quickly, looking at the scores. After the scores, he looked at the comments which were written about him. The scores were above average; the comments discussed his administrative ability and his past negligence to take control of prejudicial elements in his Division of English and the Humanities.

He appreciated the comments about the administrative aspect of the evaluation, and he knew that he was absolved of the prejudicial comments since the death of Gerald and Rutland's memorial tribute; he was not concerned.

He picked up the phone and pressed a buzzer. "Cheryl, make an appointment with the president for a discussion of my evaluation."

* * * * *

One cool, cloudless, sunny afternoon after the memorial service, Rex decided that it was a perfect day to take Marion to lunch; he took her to The Running Iron, a vintage cowboy restaurant in the village. They walked through the small, crowded courtyard, where customers sat at tables under Cinzano and Dos Equis umbrellas, to the main dining room. Coming from the bright sun into the restaurant, Marion's eyes did not adjust too quickly to the darkness. The waitress told them to sit wherever they wished. Rex led her to a table for four and sat her behind the table facing him and the restaurant, so that she was looking into the almost empty bar behind him.

When her eyes adjusted and she looked up at the ceiling, she said, "Rex, look at that!" And he heard her laugh for the first time. Suspended from the ceiling were at least a hundred pairs of old, well-worn boots, handbags from the sixties, and bicycle wheels.

"Rex, turn around. Look at the head of that wild boar at the entrance to the bar! I've never seen anything like this. It's wonderful."

"So is the food," he said.

The waitress explained the specials. Marion ordered the soup-and-half sandwich special: chicken noodle soup with homemade thread-thin noodles and half of a plump chicken-salad sandwich. Rex ordered his usual: a monstrous club sandwich accompanied by curly beer batter French fries. They both had iced tea.

"Rex, this was a wonderful idea. Just what I needed."

"Marion, the ambiance of The Running Iron makes you feel down-to-earth good, while the food just plain sends you. And that's *reeeel* cool, ma'm."

Marion threw back her head and gave the heartiest laugh in a long time.

"See. It's healing," Rex said.

"What? The food?"

"Yes." Then he added, "With the laughter."

Rex saw her eyes sparkle as she sipped her iced tea through a straw.

* * * * *

"Good to see you again, Rex," President Wilson said.

190

"It's been a busy end-of-semester."

"Sure has. And a sad one. Good teacher, Gerald."

"Damned good."

Rex sat in one of the deep green, leather-upholstered chairs in front of George's mammoth kidney-shaped cherry wood desk. It was clear of anything except an open manila folder on a huge dark green blotter, a sea captain's brass clock, and a pair of brass pens in a green marble stand.

"How are things going with the English and Humanities Division?"

"Fine. A bit quiet now. Everyone's correcting finals."

Elbows on his desk, George lifted the top sheet on the open folder.

"Your evaluation is excellent as usual. You know, you're a damned good administrator. One of the best."

Rex nodded acceptance and opened the folder on his lap.

"Thanks," he said.

"Have you read your evaluations?"

"With interest."

"Your scores are above average for your administrative functions. But there seemed to be a problem of discrimination of one kind and another."

"I know, George, but I can't put out a memo warning against discrimination. It all had to do with Rutland's and Traci's relationship. They're in love, they're living together, and they plan to be married at the end of the semester."

He paused and leaned forward.

"I still can't believe that some educated people...." He stopped speaking and made a helpless gesture with his hands. "Anyway, some things are left better unaddressed and they work themselves out, as did this situation. Don't you agree?"

He sat back again and, as he did so, the leather of the chair seemed to sigh in relief at the conclusion of his monologue.

George nodded in assent.

"These evaluations were done in early April before Gerald's death. Since Rutland made that beautiful speech about Gerald's close friendship with him, I haven't noticed any evidence of racial resentment among the faculty."

"Good. Perhaps death is sometimes a healer in more than one way. Now, how about Professor Rostrand?"

Rex felt his mouth go dry. In the evaluation packet, there had been an allusion to Lizbeth's affair and to the letters slipped under the office doors of the English faculty by Gillian's husband, Ralph.

Because Rex had anticipated some question concerning the Lizbeth incident, he had tucked a copy of the letter inside his folder and now withdrew it and handed it to George.

"Here's a copy. A number of the faculty were quite upset over it and never acknowledged it. They brought it to me."

George read it.

"I can understand his anger at the loss of his wife, but I cannot abide his low, reviling name-calling."

"That's not all." Rex said. "He sent a copy to the editor of the college newspaper who came to me about it."

"That man's sick. I always thought you had only to 'beware the wrath of a woman scorned'."

"Professor Rostrand said that she can withstand anything anyone says or does, because her students and her colleagues know her well and respect her. And for God's sake, George, this *is* the end of the twentieth century!"

"But there *are* always some medieval minds lurking out there." George continued, "I have nothing more to say about your evaluation, Rex. You know that I'm always pleased with your work and the way you handle your affairs in the Division to benefit the college. You have the largest and the most difficult Division in the college, with the most prima donnas on campus."

They laughed.

"How's your budget coming along?"

"It's the first week of May. Cheryl's typing up the rough draft for me."

"What about Gerald's replacement?"

"We're interviewing. Actually, with the way the enrollment is growing, I'll need four new full-time faculty."

"Ask for them and budget them. I'll see to it that you get them. You know, Rex, I'd like to see more African Americans or Asians in the English Department." He stopped. "Or maybe someone of another life style?"

"Frankly, George, we have a few closeted people who have now just come out to me since they received Ralph Warner's letter."

"Interesting."

"And you, as I did, would think they were straight."

"I don't want to know."

Rex laughed. "And I'd never tell you."

George smiled.

"You know, George, I went to a parochial school when I was young and endured unbelievable physical torture that would set the media afire with screams of child abuse. But, you know, I thank that woman, Sister Angela, a nun, for making me who I am today. She taught me virtues that I could only have learned by way of her harsh and cruel treatment. She said that I'd never amount to anything. I wish she could see me today. You told me that I'm a good administrator and...."

"One of the best. College president material, I'd say."

"Thanks again. But you know the virtues which she taught me that helped to make me the best?"

Rex spoke reverently now. "Obedience, patience, understanding, forgiveness, and tolerance."

"I'm not Catholic, but I'd say she was a saint."

"I've never forgotten her. She has come to mind many times during my career. Naturally, without knowing it then because of my youth, I have realized over the years that she has made me a better person."

He stopped for a moment to take a deep sigh.

"Her lessons have helped me to be more tolerant of Lizbeth's lifestyle. I must confess to you that I'm in love with her."

George looked at him and then dropped his eyes and said, "I'm sorry."

Rex stood.

"I can wait. Sister taught me tolerance and patience, don't forget."

George came around to Rex, took his hand and simultaneously patted him on the shoulder.

"You're a great guy. Remember that. She'll come around and make you happy someday, I hope. I'll pray."

Rex covered George's hand with his.

"Saint Anthony, I hope."

"Whoever."
"He's great."
They laughed and Rex left.

* * * * *

At one o'clock Marion went to the mailbox at the end of the driveway. There were solicitous letters from mortuaries and stone carvers. There was one other envelope; she looked at the return address. The letter was from Sarah Kendrick.

Inside, she sat on the sofa and opened the letter.

> May 5th
>
> My dear Marion,
>
> Forgive me for not calling, but I felt that a phone call would have been too impersonal at such a tragic time; I wish I could have visited with you, but I didn't have the emotional strength. Knowing how you and Gerald adored each other and how you lived for each other has torn me apart. I have cried for you until I can't shed another tear. To offer you my sympathy is shallow, when to offer you my heart is what I really wish I could do.
>
> Edward told me about the beautiful SGA tribute at the Grade. I wish I could have been there.
>
> Because you were with me when I needed you, I so often wished I could have been with you. If I could, I would do so this moment. If you're receiving friends, call me, and Edward will bring me. I'd love to hear from you and to spend time with you.
>
> Since the last time we spoke, Edward has changed back to his attentive and loving self, and we are once more enjoying our marriage.
>
> Affectionately,
> Sarah

194

Marion folded the letter and tucked it into the envelope before she placed it on the coffee table; she sat for a minute musing on what Sarah had written; she was happy for Sarah and smiled as she remembered their last conversation about men and their version of menopause. Deep in thought, she almost jumped when the phone rang on the end table beside her.

"Yes, this is Professor Ritchey's home. No, he's not here. Who's calling?"

Marion felt her heart stop for a minute before it skipped into a more rapid beat. She listened intently, then she said, "This is Mrs. Ritchey. My husband was killed in an accident three weeks ago. Could you give me your name again and your number? I'll have a friend call you to talk about this?"

She jotted the name and number on the pad by the phone.

"Goodbye."

She dialed Rex at his office and Cheryl put her through immediately.

"Rex, I just received a call from the chief editor at Crispin and Crispin. They want to publish Gerald's book."

She burst into tears and couldn't stop crying. When she was finally able to talk again, she said, "I have her name and phone number. It's after four in New York. She told me that she'll be there until six. I told her about Gerald and that I would have a friend call to talk with her."

When she gave the information to Rex, he assured her that he would call immediately and get back to her. She placed the handset down and began to cry again as she murmured Gerald's name.

* * * * *

Rex received the contract by FedEx within a week. He called Marion to tell her that he would drop it off at his attorney's office for approval. His attorney had worked on other authors' contracts from small publishing houses because they weren't always in the authors' best interests. He told her he'd call her and the two of them would go to the attorney's office to sign or not to sign.

Marion mentioned that the crematorium called to tell her that Mr. Ritchey was ready to come home. She could barely say the words.

"And Rex, we'll pick an urn when we go there."

She hesitated a second, then added, "Rex, when you have time, would you and Rutland come over and take Gerald's clothes to the community church?"

He agreed and said that he would get in touch with Rutland. They would concur on a day, probably this coming Saturday.

"Oh, and Rex, one more thing. Would you go into Gerald's study with me? I haven't been in there since...."

She couldn't finish the sentence.

* * * * *

The semester ended the third week of May, and the private life of everyone took on new meaning. Some of the faculty made preparations to teach summer classes, others made plans for camping outings at national parks, for motor trips, or for trips abroad.

Rex took Marion to the crematorium and, for Gerald's remains, she chose a hand-carved wooden chest designed as if it were a stack of three books. She wanted Gerald's name engraved in gold down the spine of the center book. The attendant said that there would be a three-week delay and that the remains of Mr. Ritchey would be placed in the chest.

From Pacific Grove they drove to the attorney's office in Monterey. Lowell Sweeney came from behind his desk and Marion extended her hand. He was a strikingly lean and handsome man with a full head of wavy gray hair who certainly did not look to be seventy as Rex had told her.

They sat down.

He walked around and sat at his desk.

"Mrs. Ritchey, without an agent to fend for you, the contract from Crispin and Crispin is generous and quite in order. It seems that for a first and only novel they are expecting a landslide of advance orders. Of course, I'm sure they will exploit the fact that it's a posthumously published novel."

He smiled, then continued.

"You're too young to remember Richard Lockridge who wrote *Raintree County*, but perhaps you read about John Kennedy Toole who wrote *A Confederacy of Dunces*. Both committed suicide before their books were accepted and published. The publishers cashed in on their suicides and both books were bestsellers. *Raintree County* was even a movie with a young Elizabeth Taylor.

"In the contract, they've done an unusual thing as publishers. They have listed their tentative advertising campaign in the major papers: a full page in the *New York Times Book Review*, quarter pages in *The Washington Post, The Boston Globe, The Atlanta Constitution, The Chicago Tribune, The L.A. Times*, and *The San Francisco Chronicle*. Of course, they're all aimed at Christmas sales which they're expecting to be fantastic because of the advance publicity I'm sure they're planning. An initial printing of a hundred thousand copies for a first and only novel is the dream of most productive living novelists."

"So, what does Marion do now?"

"She just signs it and keeps the bottom copy."

Lowell handed the contract and a pen across the desk to Marion who leaned over and signed it.

"We'll put it in the mail today."

"Thank you, Mr. Sweeney."

"Thanks, Lowell."

"My pleasure, Rex."

They shook hands and Rex ushered Marion out of the office.

* * * * *

Traci and Rutland set the date of June tenth for their wedding.

Rex was notified that the proofs for the book would arrive by late August. The editor at Crispin and Crispin said she would write the blurb for the fall book list which gives advance notice to book chains and booksellers.

* * * * *

After work one afternoon, Michael Larson drove to see Sheila and found a *Garage Apartment for Rent* sign at the entrance to her driveway. The rental agent's number was below the announcement.

* * * * *

St. Mary's By-The-Sea Episcopal Church—the first church in Pacific Grove—was built in 1887 of clear grained redwood, a common building material at the time. The architects had made use of local woods—pine, cedar, fir, and walnut—to create a uniquely warm, aesthetic interior.

Promptly at five o'clock, Rex and Rutland came out of the sacristy and stood at the foot of the three carpeted Trinity steps. Rutland wore a tux and Rex wore a dark blue double-breasted suit with a light blue shirt and a navy tie with small, light-blue stripes. Both wore a blush-tipped white rosebud in their lapels. The priest stood on the top step smiling down at Rex and Rutland and looking up the aisle toward the marble baptismal font in the rear of the church in anticipation of Traci's entrance.

The organist started to play and sing "All I ask of you" from *Phantom of the Opera*.

Marion, Lizbeth, and Gillian turned in their pew to watch Traci walk slowly down the aisle in keeping with the beauty of the music and the declaration of love within the words. The organist sang the words, not with the same unmatchable superstar quality of Barbra Streisand, but as meaningfully. The three women couldn't resist crying: Marion for the loss of the man to whom she had been devoted, Lizbeth and Gillian for themselves and for sharing with Traci and Rutland this joyous moment and the heart-pleading words of a lover.

Traci seemed to be bathed in a halo of radiance; her knee-length creamy satin dress was cut low and ended with shoulder puffs; full-length arm-hugging sleeves stopped in a gentle vee just before her middle finger. She carried a nosegay of blush-tinged off-white rosebuds. Rutland's ring was tied loosely with a white ribbon to one of the rosebuds; at ring exchange time, it could be slipped easily off the ribbon and onto his finger. Her hair was swept to the side, her face was delicately made up. She smiled and winked in her conspiratorially impish way at the three women as she passed their pew.

As Traci approached the altar, Rex stepped forward. The music stopped and the priest greeted them.

When the question was asked "Who gives this woman to be wed?" Rex answered and handed Traci to Rutland; they smiled at each other with a display of love that even the priest commented on.

Rex stepped back and saw the pair bathed in the colored light of the stained glass East Window depicting the Annunciation to Mary by the Angel Gabriel. Mary was seated on a stone chair; behind her was the expanse of Monterey Bay as seen from the front of the church.

Vows and rings were exchanged. They kissed. Marion, Lizbeth, Gillian, and Rex applauded as the priest pronounced them husband and wife.

The organ boomed out joyously as Traci and Rutland turned and walked up the aisle, followed by the four wedding guests.

On a table in the porch entry, Lizbeth had set three florist's cones of rose petals as she entered the church for the service. When Traci and Rutland started down the steps, they called to them to stop. All three women showered them with rose petals.

Marion rode with Rex; Lizbeth and Gillian followed; the wedding party went to The French Poodle in Carmel for a champagne dinner.

Traci and Rutland left for San Francisco the next morning and flew to London. They would be away for six weeks: London, Paris, Rome, Vienna, and Budapest. When they returned, they would live at their apartment until they found a house in the valley.

* * * * *

Marion was in the kitchen preparing lunch when she heard a truck pull into the driveway. The knocker sounded before she had a chance to open the door. The FedEx delivery woman greeted her and had her sign the sheet on the clipboard. Then she handed Marion the carton.

"It's heavy, Mrs. Ritchey."

"Thank you," Marion said as she took it. "It sure is, but I can handle it."

She closed the door and took the carton into the kitchen. It was from Crispin and Crispin.

What date is this? she thought. *November eighth.*

She took a butcher knife from the sink drawer and pried open the carton. Inside was a letter and six copies of Gerald's novel. A chill ran through her at the sight of the title and his name.

She shivered.

Tears flooded her eyes.

She carried the open carton into the living room and set it on the coffee table. She blinked away the tears and wiped her eyes as she read the brief letter which informed her that advance sales were even better than anticipated. Her six author's copies were enclosed and they hoped she liked the packaging.

Packaging? What do they mean?

The editor closed, wishing her happy holidays.

She gently lifted out a copy. The dust jacket was a sea of puffy white clouds against a blue sky; the title, *Come Back, My Love,* was printed in dark blue windswept letters. Gerald's name was at the bottom in the same dark blue windswept letters.

If the dust jacket was packaging, then the packaging was exquisite.

She opened the book and had to blink the tears away so she could read the synopsis of the story on the dust jacket; it was continued on the inside of the back jacket flap. Beneath the blurb was the photo of a smiling Gerald taken last March in Santa Barbara. Under his picture, she read:

> Gerald Ritchey died in an auto accident in April. He is survived by his wife, Marion, who lives in Carmel Valley, California.

Marion put the book on the coffee table, took three of them and laid them flat on the mantelpiece as if they were bookends holding up Gerald's remains. She took two more and set them on the other side. She sat on the sofa and opened the book. She came to the dedication page which she had never seen. When she read it, she sobbed deeply and her heart pounded—as if it wanted to escape from the cage of her breast; she clasped the open book hard against it.

For Marion
my life, my love, my heart, my soul

Aloud, as if the words were wrenched from her, she half wept, half moaned, "Oh, Gerald, come back, my love."

About the Author

John Bodnar was born in Pittsburgh, Pennsylvania. While working at Kaufmann's Department Store for several years as menswear copywriter, he attended Duquesne University for his Bachelor's Degree, and received his Master's Degree in English at Shippensburg University where he was asked to join the faculty.

At Prince George's Community College in Maryland, he was Professor of English, the Chairman, and then Associate Dean of English Studies while he worked on his Ph.D. Associate at the University of Maryland.

He has published numerous articles and poetry.

Mr. Bodnar has lived in Pittsburgh and Shippensburg, PA; Washington, DC; Carmel Valley, California; and now resides in Las Vegas, Nevada.

He is at work on the sequel to *Come Back, My Love.*